For Team Aran.
The most magic collection of pals.
All my love.

Angus Mcnab
Scott Alcorn
Kathy Burns
Kiri Gillespie
Megan Lancaster
Julia Cox
Tiffy Shedden
Colin Shedden
Hebe Shedden
Willow Shedden
Trish Ross
Hector Lancaster
Jess Moses
Annalee Donnaghy
Anna Walker
Gillian Ramsay
Justin Tunstall
Will Verdino
Anna Jauncey
Kirsty Fisher

And also for James, who has put up with us all.

ARAN

RECIPES AND STORIES
FROM A BAKERY IN THE HEART
OF SCOTLAND

FLORA SHEDDEN

PHOTOGRAPHY BY

LAURA EDWARDS

Hardie Grant

BOOKS

SEEDED BREAD   CIABATTA / FOCACCIA

kg   WHITE FLOUR
.5kg   GRANARY   3.1 Kg   FLOUR (NORMAL
75gm   SALT   2.8 2.9 kg WATER   BREAD ONE)
50gm   YEAST   60g   SALT
2.1 Kg WATER   50g   YEAST
3.6 Kg POOLISH   80-100g OLIVE OIL
        400gm SEEDS   5.57

ROLLS   Garlic Bread

1 kg   WHITE FLOUR
1 kg   GRANARY
40g   SALT
40g   YEAST
1.3kg   WATER

12:45

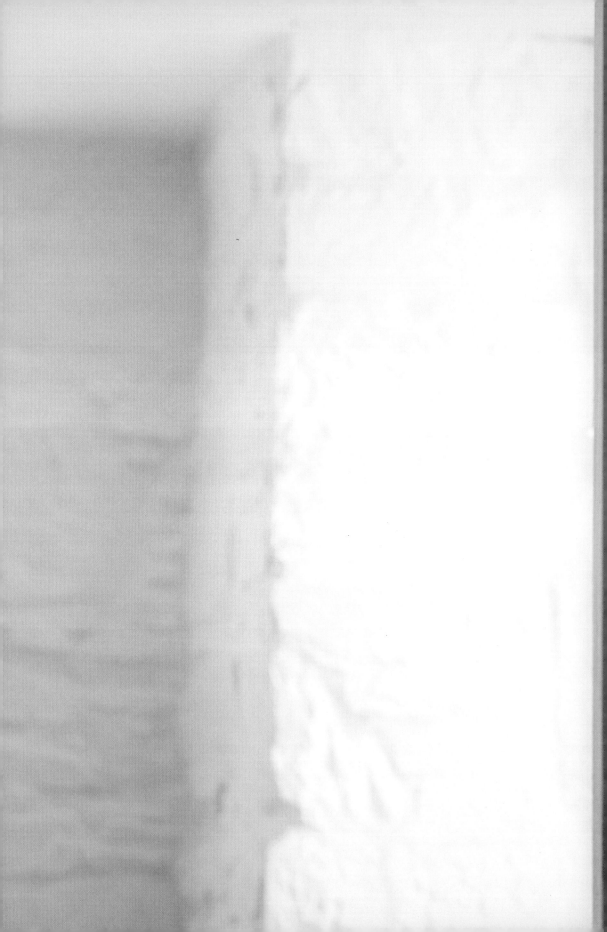

INTRODUCTION

It was a little over three years ago, on a *dreich* (dreary) Saturday afternoon – spent in the pub, of course – that the concept of Aran was first discussed. Perhaps a little intoxicated and consequently wittering a stream of nonsense, my fairly new boyfriend, James, introduced me to Angus, a colleague of his who he often described simply as 'the best person he knew'. I wittered some more nonsense and we eventually got on to the topic of baking. Angus revealed he had a 'bread shed': a place where he would create loaves upon loaves post-work and early in the morning. I immediately became jealous of this magic little set-up, having spent the last few months searching for my own wee flour oasis. We agreed that we would talk further about a more serious venture, ideally including bricks and mortar, something a bit more permanent than a shed. It was both the first time I had seriously considered opening a bakery, and also the first time I had met anyone mad enough to agree to do it with me.

Angus and I continued to discuss various concepts and ideas for months afterwards. Of course, this involved touching on some of my more wholly idiotic plans, after which he would both politely and sensibly stop me going any further. He remains an expert in that particular field to this day.

Despite all of our scheming, we remained at a loss when it came to a location. Dunkeld is a small town, and ultimately has a limited variety of shops. I was subscribed to every property website available and sending regular emails to those locals who were always in the know.

NO. 2 ATHOLL STREET

One October morning, on a last-minute family trip to the south of Spain – ironically a holiday I had only agreed to go on because I had given up all hope when it came to our scheming – my phone buzzed. No. 2 Atholl Street was up for sale. We flew back a few days later, on a Monday morning, and by 3 p.m. that day we were standing in the abandoned building; a small shop space on the ground floor with a flat covering the first and second floor. It was impossible to view properly as a lack of power meant we could barely see the dark and crumbling interiors, and the low winter sun and Scottish afternoon light didn't help us much either. My main memories are of the old tobacco dispenser – in a previous life, the shop space had been a newsagent – and the burgundy curtains from the previous owner which still hung in the living room directly above. I had longed for a wee shop to rent, but this was a building with a flat – arguably a house – and it was only on the market to buy.

A few more viewings, this time with a torch, an architect and a lawyer in tow, and we decided to go for it. In hindsight, this was madness. I was 20, self-employed, and had known James, who was to buy the building with me, for no more than five months. Between the two of us we had a princely sum of zero savings. I scraped together a business plan and miraculously received approval for a commercial mortgage. On the day of my 21st birthday, our lawyer phoned to say it was ours. Long and tedious legal issues drew out proceedings excessively, but two days before Christmas of that same year, I drove to Perth to collect the keys. As 2016 came to an end, I had the daunting prospect of starting a business, renovating a shop and trying to cobble together some form of a home for myself and James, a man I still considered a fairly new addition to my life. I drank quite a lot that Hogmanay.

Nearly a year to the day that I got the phone call in Spain, 19 October 2017, we opened the doors of Aran. My mum and I, our hands both rough after months and months of painting, sanding, bad attempts at plastering, tiling and endless trips to the skip, along with Angus and James, and Scott and Megan – old school friends who jumped on board once we got the building – were all behind the counter that first day. Even my littlest sister Willow, aged 13, was there to help. We sold out in four hours.

A lot has changed since those early days, but our customers haven't. They have been the key to Aran's success, taking our hand and steering us in the right direction. Frankly, we were clueless in those first few weeks and months, working late into the night and then getting up at the crack of dawn to do it all over again. Our customers asked for more varieties of sourdough, so we made all our breads sourdough, bar one. They wanted lunch and savoury treats, so we did our very best to create mountains of sandwiches and salads, although we still often run out. They wanted real plates and crockery, so we bought them. But most of all, they wanted us to keep going. That alone was enough to survive the carnage that was our first year of trading.

Three months, nay, three weeks after opening, we knew we were too short on space. We had done our best with what was a tiny wee space, and it was all we could afford at the time, but alas, it still wasn't enough. During our Christmas break, I set about scouring the village and surrounding area for extra production space. As usual, our customers came up trumps and sent endless ideas, offers of garages, unused outbuildings and even a stable at one point. It was heart-warming and generous to say the least. Eventually, we found an old veterinary practice a mile away in Birnam. Come summer, after many a hiccup (no thanks to a certain large power company), we were up and running on a far grander scale.

With the production kitchen fully functioning, the way our days panned out changed drastically. There was enough worktop space to make croissants through the day, something that was previously an evening task. We had more oven space, and suddenly were able to bake cakes and bread at the same time – with the previous set-up, that would have resulted in a cake so burnt you could use it for charcoal. We had to relearn our whole day-to-day system.

DAILY RITUALS

Baking is so much about time, and time of day. It can also be about capturing the time in the day, savouring little moments to yourself. Bread will always be best when baked fresh in the wee hours of the morning, and there is something about the promise of this that makes commencing the process a whole 24 hours prior far easier to set about. The smell of hot butter and baking croissants will for me always be associated with a weekend morning, the sort where pyjamas remain your outfit of choice well into the day. Loaf cakes are best enjoyed mid-morning, cuppa in hand, and ideally with something equally delicious to read. Fancy cakes are often reserved for late in the afternoon, maybe even paired with a glass of something special, enjoyed as part of a high or afternoon tea. My point here being that baked goods always have their own place and time. They capture memories of that day, or that hour, and tend to remind me of previous meals eaten and enjoyed in a similar light.

Both this book and the Aran lifestyle revolves around this concept of time and the rhythm it can bring to your day to day life. We bake to match it, and try to keep in tune with it. I suppose it is more instinctive that way.

Aran has been nothing if not a learning curve, and in some ways that has come full circle with this book. All of our recipes in the beginning were designed to be cooked in a domestic kitchen. I had no experience of anything else, no fancy equipment, only broken spatulas and favourite but slightly blunt knives, much like all home cooks. Commercial kit scared me, and we didn't have much of it in the early days. It didn't take long, however, for us to learn that in order to keep our shop stocked after 10 a.m., we were going to have to scale it up a bit. Angus was far better at this than I was, but I cottoned on eventually. Ironically, while writing this book, I have now gone back the other way. I have questioned all of our recipes, ingredients and methods extensively. I scaled back and adapted them to the way they were originally written, the way they were when I would potter around my mum's kitchen making a mess at 10 p.m. for no reason other than sheer enjoyment, and in order to have the promise of cake the next day.

You should bake from this book in order to feed hunger, feed friends, feed your family. These recipes should be tackled in order to celebrate occasions and heal any losses, they should be made because it's a Tuesday afternoon and why not? Ultimately, it should be for the satisfaction of smiles on faces, be it your own or a loved one.

SENSE IN SIMPLICITY

Sugar gets a bad rep nowadays, as does gluten, sadly. In the world of food trends, diets, rules and regs, there is nothing but confusion, particularly surrounding the sweet and the stodgy. My principles remain the same throughout this bizarre time. Use proper and honest ingredients, and, more importantly, ones that you can pronounce without consulting a scientist. Think of food as a source of fuel and satisfaction, not as something to fear or discuss negatively. Life is a balancing act, and your plate shouldn't be any different. Treats, as the word suggests, are for eating, and I reckon for appreciating. As with every recipe in this book, we believe they should be prepared with just as much love and affection as you feel while consuming them. There is no harm in indulging from time to time. Cooking should be celebratory and bountiful – let's not do it half-heartedly.

It's not only food groups that get discussed widely nowadays – technique and terminology chat seems to be all the rage when it comes to food, and even more so for baking. To be frank, I find all the language surrounding it excessive, and in most cases best ignored. Sourdough has been made for thousands of years, baked over fires initially. I suspect that if they managed back then without the additional complication of specific vernacular and terms such as 'bulk fermentation' and 'levain', then we will be okay too. The reality is that these books are often written by professionals that have spent hours honing their craft and practising using kilos and kilos of flour. Single loaves are often an alien concept. There is of course nothing wrong with learning from 'the best'; however, it doesn't translate too well for a home kitchen at times. I have never received any sort of training and learnt everything I know using domestic equipment and from pottering around and practising at home. I am very much a home cook, and proud to be. This provides a lot of amusement to a dear friend,

Will Verdino, who is a professional. He once commented on my lack of qualifications in jest and we have since referred to him as the 'PTC' – professionally trained chef. When it comes to bread and cakes, all too often it has little to do with the technical terminology and accuracy, and more to do with the enjoyment of those baking.

For me, it doesn't have anything to do with alchemy. Baking should be about instinct, and I truly believe the more you listen to your own gut feeling the more you will improve. We don't approach bread as a desperate search for the perfect loaf. Breads should be delicious and moreish, caramelised crusts crackling and singing when they come out of the oven, as if to say 'I am ready'. Baking has far more to do with scent and sound than visuals. Aesthetics regularly come second. When you work in a bakery, you survive solely on the ugly forgotten loaves that decided to cook a little squint, or the ones that tore open along the side as opposed to where they were scored. A lot of the time I don't put these out on the shelves, mainly as they tend not to sell, sadly, but also because those are the tastiest of the lot in my opinion. My loaves looked slightly crooked for three years when I first started baking, and I sort of loved them for it. Trust me, some of the best bread you will eat will more often than not be the lopsided-looking loaves, and there is absolutely nothing wrong with that.

IT TAKES A VILLAGE

People are at the heart of everything we do. Two years in and with a team more than triple the size of our humble beginnings, I feel very lucky that I get to blether away with Team Aran every day. There is much hilarity and many post-shift drinks, but there is also a lot of bloody hard work. Our days don't end quite as late as they used to, thank god, but our working hours remain longer than most. My mum used to say catering is a thankless job, and on bad days I can agree with her, but most days I lose track of the times I hear the words 'thank you'. For me, that is enough.

We have been so charmed by our customers. Some swap stories over the counter, some leave us falling about on the floor with laughter, some even come to check up on us. Some fight in jest over the last sausage roll, and some buy bread and coffees for strangers. More than anyone else, I owe a huge debt of gratitude to Aran's customers. To the sweet-toothed among them who inhale our goods and leave with a smile and spring in their step; to the hungry kids who tackle croissants larger than their own heads with nothing but eagerness; to the more reserved customer who tries something new for the first time; and to those who come through the door on a regular basis just to make us chuckle. You are all marvellous and we are so grateful.

A huge thanks is also due to our Crowdfunders, without whom we wouldn't have made it this far. When it became apparent that we had bitten off more than we could chew financially, we turned to our community and were met with nothing but love and generosity. The bakery truly wouldn't be standing upright without you. This story is as much down to every one of you as it is to those that work hard here every day. Thank you from the bottom of our hearts.

With love,

Flora

NOTES

*Read this before you start to make
any of the recipes.*

WEIGHTS

For all recipes we recommend weighing everything in grams with electric scales. It is the most accurate way to cook and bake and can be crucial when it comes to the smaller things, such as yeast and salt. We also endorse weighing liquids in grams, too. Not only does this improve the exactness of a recipe but it also minimises washing up, which is always something to be grateful for. For liquids that have the same consistency as water (for example, milk), their weight in grams will be the same as their volume in ml, so this is easily interchangeable. Denser liquids, such as cream and yoghurt, will weigh slightly more than their volume, so we suggest following the recipes and weighing as listed. Simply zero your scales and pour away. Never will you need to scrape out another measuring jug again! Importantly, for a sourdough starter, the more active it is, the less it will weigh, due to the fact that it will contain more gas. A slightly less active starter will weigh a lot more despite filling up the same cup size. For this reason, we have left cup measurements out altogether for quantities when using the sourdough starter (see pages 26–27) to make your bread, as they will be particularly inaccurate.

FLOUR

This, I would argue, is the most important ingredient you will need as a baker. Take your time to research and look into different millers and also the different varieties. Experiment with different varieties of the same type of flour. The best way to do this is, of course, to bake with them. Only you will be able to decide what you like the best. Once you have found a variety or a miller you like, we recommend not changing your flour or supplier too regularly. The more you bake, the more you will get a feel for the specific flour and its unique qualities. This is important in order to improve and move forward with your baking. I would also add that varieties are not interchangeable. If a recipe requires strong bread flour, do not use plain (all-purpose) flour and vice versa. There are certain volumes of protein in each different flour, and these will affect the final consistency of your bake. For example, a cookie made with strong bread flour will be far tougher in texture as opposed to one made with plain flour.

We have been using Marriages flour since we started Aran, and rate not only its quality and consistency, but also the company's ethics. It was important for us to use British-grown wheat. Other companies I would recommend are Carrs, Mungoswells Mill, Scotland the Bread, Doves, Shipton Mill, Aberfeldy Mill and Blair Atholl Mill.

SALT

Salt is crucial in both sweet and savoury bakes. It helps with not only flavour but also the structure of bakes. When it comes to bread, make sure it is included with the first knead of the dough. Do not add it afterwards, as all too often it ruins the consistency and texture of the bread. Dough without salt will more often than not overprove. For doughs and cakes, we tend to use fine salt, ideally unrefined. For any doughs or cakes that contain butter we use unsalted butter. This is important as different brands vary their percentage of salt, and this can lead to small inconsistencies. When baking with sugar, you need to be careful with the salt addition, and using unsalted butter allows you to add to taste. For topping focaccia, or making cookies and biscuits, we use flaky salt, preferably Maldon.

WATER

As you will see, we weigh all our liquids in grams for accuracy – and also to avoid more washing up. There is nothing better than Scottish tap water, particularly around these parts. I suppose we are biased though. There shouldn't be a difference in flavour or consistency, no matter where you are. All water used is straight-from-the-tap temperature unless otherwise stated.

YEAST

There is nae snobbery here when it comes to yeast. We adore sourdough, but accept that some people need to give their gnashers a break and on some occasions opt for a softer loaf. Use dried instant action yeast, or fresh yeast if you can get hold of it. All of our recipes specify dried instant action. To use fresh, simply multiply the quantity by three. So, for example, if a recipe calls for 7 g (1 generous teaspoon) instant yeast, you will require 21 g (1½ tablespoons) fresh yeast.

HEAT

All ovens vary in their cooking temperatures so you need to get to know yours, check with the manufacturer's instructions and, if necessary, use an oven thermometer. The recipes in this book have been tested in a fan-assisted oven at the given temperatures, but these should be treated as a guide only. If you are cooking in a conventional, non-fan-assisted oven, you should increase the temperatures by 10-20°C (50-60°F/Gas 2).

1. ARAN

Bread, through the night

Scottish Gaelic, masc. noun, from the Old Irish arán, *meaning 1. bread, loaf*

We start our day with freshly baked bread at the crack of dawn, even before the birds are singing. It seemed fitting to do the same here.

SOUR

FOR STARTERS

Nine times out of ten I read sourdough recipes that ask, in a very casual fashion, for you to make your own starter. 'In 2–3 days you will be able to bake with it…'

Reader, this has not been my experience.

It took me seven attempts to create a truly active starter, and even then it wasn't ready to bake within three days. I think my first successful one was more than a week old when I determined that it was ready to go. Please bear this in mind before kicking off your sourdough education. There are a lot of learning curves early on, and none of them as frustrating as an inactive starter.

If you don't have a huge amount of experience with bread, I would seek out your local baker and ask for some of their starter. We give away loads of the stuff at Aran, and are more than happy to do so. Our starter is called Big Mumma, and we hope that all the 'Little Mummas' we give to our eager customers will become a member of their family. Your starter is a living breathing thing. It needs to be fed and watered just like the rest of us.

On the other hand, if you do have the time and patience required, I would recommend giving your own starter a go. The process itself is simple. Once established and regularly fed, it can be very reliable.

ACTIVE STARTER

In a bowl, weigh out 100 g (3½ oz/scant ½ cup) water with 100 g (3½ oz/¾ cup) strong white bread flour. Mix together, then transfer to a glass jar or clear plastic container. Visibility is key, so you can see any bubbles forming. Cover and leave for 24 hours at room temperature.

The following day, feed your starter the same 100 g (3½ oz/scant ½ cup) water and 100 g (3½ oz/¾ cup) strong white bread flour. Mix and cover again for 24 hours at room temperature.

On the third day, you should hopefully see some bubbles appearing, although don't be disheartened if they are only small. Rome wasn't built in a day. Pour away half of your starter and feed with the same quantities again.

Repeat this step on the fourth day: pouring away half and feeding.

By the fifth day, your bubbles should be a bit more consistent and the mixture should have grown in size since its last feed. Repeat the feeding process.

On the sixth day, if you are happy with the aroma (sour, but not painfully so; there should be a beer-like scent) and the appearance (bubbly and light), you are ready to bake with it. If you are still unsure, there is no harm in waiting a few days.

If there is no sign of life at all after six or seven days, bin the starter and begin again. This is not a failure on your part (unless you have ignored it completely), but rather a lack of good bacteria and yeasts. Just pray for better luck when it comes to your bugs and naturally occurring bacteria.

Once up and running, feed your starter daily, although you can cut down the quantities by half. If you don't bake with it everyday, throw away some of your starter each time you feed it. This means that you won't end up with mountains of the stuff, but also, more importantly, that you are incorporating more weight than the weight of the existing starter. For example, if your existing starter is weighing in at 150 g (5½ oz), you should either feed it at the very least 75 g (2¾ oz/⅓ cup) water and 75 g (2¾ oz/⅔ cup) flour – ideally more – or throw some away to make the initial weight 50 g (1¾ oz). That way, you can get away with feeding it only 25 g (1 oz/1½ tablespoons) water and 25 g (1 oz/1½ tablespoons) flour. If it breaks your heart to see it go, remember you can use any excess starter in the Sour crumpets recipe on page 101, as you can use both active and 'starved' starter to make them.

If you plan to go away on holiday, or just want a break from baking, simply move your starter to the refrigerator. It will last for two weeks untouched, or a month if fed once a week. When you want to start baking again, bring it out from the refrigerator and give it two big feeds, or until it becomes active and bubbly again.

If you totally neglect your starter, as we all do sometimes, and discover a lovely black liquid has formed on top (it's called hooch, and I think is my favourite term in the ridiculous bakers' language), then don't worry. Simply pour the majority away and feed it with 25 g (1 oz/ 1½ tablespoons) water and 25 g (1 oz/1½ tablespoons) flour. Over the next three days, work your way up to a feed of 100 g (3½ oz/scant ½ cup) water and 100 g (3½ oz/¾ cup) flour, or until you have an active, happy starter again. It is important to take your time with this, as often a large feed can cause stress and kill off any remaining yeast in a neglected starter.

THE WETTER THE BETTER

When it comes to sourdough, we always aim for 60–70 per cent hydration as a minimum. This means that for every 60–70 g (2–2½ oz/¼–⅓ cup) water in a recipe, there is 100 g (3½ oz/¾ cup) flour. When calculating this, however, you need to bear in mind that there are equal parts water and flour in your starter. Here's an example:

200 g (7 oz/¾ cup) water
75 g (2¾ oz) Active starter (opposite)
325 g (11½ oz/2¾ cups) strong white bread flour

This recipe breaks down as 237.5 g (8⅓ oz/1 scant cup) water and 362.5g (12¾ oz/3 cups) flour. This means you have a 65 per cent hydration. The more water you can get into your dough, the better; however, there is a fine balance when it comes to shaping and handling your dough. There is a reason that focaccia (90 per cent hydration) is baked free form on a flat sheet, as opposed to in a bread basket. If you do incorporate more water, you will find it requires more kneading in order to build up the gluten bonds and form a stronger structure for shaping.

THE WHITE STUFF

Try to stick with one variety of flour. Most bread flours make good bread, and an experienced baker will adjust the formula and times to suit the flour; however, you need to have consistency to achieve this skill. This relies on the starter, too. As stated on page 18 in the section on flour, the best way to become experienced is to repeat your bake and replicate your ingredients again and again. With no variables, you will start to get a good feel for the dough and the starter and how your own actions and methods affect the overall outcome as opposed to the ingredients.

CLASSIC

As with all things, it is important to start simply. This is our most simple loaf, but also our biggest seller in the bakery. The best thing since before sliced bread. You will need a *banneton*, or proving basket, for this recipe. See recipe picture overleaf.

Makes 1 loaf

200 g (7 oz/¾ cup) water
75 g (2½ oz) Active starter (see page 26)
325 g (11½ oz/2¾ cups) strong white bread flour, plus extra to dust
10 g (2 teaspoons) salt
semolina, to dust

Begin by mixing together the water, starter, flour and salt in a large bowl and knead together until just combined. Scrape any excess dough off your hands and place back into the bowl. Tip the dough onto a lightly oiled work surface, scraping out any excess in order to leave a clean bowl (you will need this later).

Use the heel of your hand to push the dough away from you and into the work surface. Pull back to form a rough ball and repeat this stretching and tearing technique in order to build up the gluten. You want to do this for roughly 10 minutes, until the dough becomes stronger and has a smooth and elastic consistency. The best way to test if your dough is ready is to perform the windowpane test. Take a small amount of dough and stretch out using both hands. You are looking to form a thin film of dough that light can shine through. If the dough breaks early on or forms a hole easily, the gluten hasn't been developed enough and the dough requires another bout of stretching and tearing. Once the dough passes the windowpane test, it is ready to prove.

Lightly oil the bowl from earlier and place the dough inside. Cover with cling film (plastic wrap) and set aside in a warm environment for 2–4 hours or until noticeably grown in size. During this period, you can fold the dough. Folding the dough is the best way to build up even more gluten and helps to incorporate air during the bulk prove. It also improves your oven spring (the height of the loaf) when it comes to baking. To fold the dough, grab the edge of the dough furthest from you and pull up, stretching it, before folding over to meet the edge of the dough nearest to you. Rotate the bowl 90 degrees and repeat the same process. Do this twice more so that you have folded the dough four times in total. Finally, flip the dough so the seams are at the bottom. We repeat this technique 2–3 times during the prove, but encourage you not too fret too much about forgetting or doing more or less. It should be fun, not regimental!

The dough is proved when it is nearly double the size. Tip back onto your work surface, again lightly oiled to prevent the dough from sticking. Shape the dough into a tight ball. The easiest way to do this is to cup both hands then use them to tuck both sides of the dough underneath until your pinkies meet. Rotate the dough 90 degrees and repeat until you have a tight ball. Allow to rest for 10 minutes. This relaxes the dough and makes it easier to form your final shape.

For your final shape, lightly flour the top of your rounded dough, then tip over so it is seam-side up. Flatten the dough to form a rough square. Fold the top right corner into the middle, followed by the top left corner. Continue to fold the sides in on themselves, alternating left and right. You should end up with a rough rectangle. Using your thumbs, fold the top of the dough over itself, pressing with your thumbs to secure it. Repeat this action again, using your thumbs to secure the dough, until you end up with a tight oval shape, seam-side down. Lightly flour the top and place seam side-up into a lined banneton (proving basket). Allow to prove at room temperature for a further 2 hours before placing in the refrigerator overnight.

About 30 minutes before baking, remove the dough from the refrigerator in order to recover. Preheat your oven to 230°C (445°F/Gas 9). Place a baking stone or cast iron casserole dish (Dutch oven) in the oven to preheat also.

Once the oven has come to temperature and the dough has been allowed to warm up for 30 minutes, you are ready to bake. Dust the seam side of your dough with semolina. Carefully remove the hot stone or pan from the oven. Gently tip the dough onto the hot surface and, working fast, score down the middle of the loaf at a 45-degree angle. We use a serrated knife for this job. If using a cast iron casserole dish, place the lid back on top and slide into the oven. Bake for 25 minutes before removing the lid and baking for a further 5–10 minutes, until dark in colour and hollow sounding when tapped. If using a baking stone, return to the oven quickly and chuck a handful of ice cubes onto the base of the oven to create steam. Close the door quickly to stop any steam escaping. Bake for 25 minutes before opening the door and turning the loaf for an even colour, if required. Bake for a further 5–10 minutes until dark in colour and hollow sounding when tapped.

Allow to cool completely before slicing.

Classic sourdough

COUNTRY

This is a wonderfully flexible loaf, and arguably my personal favourite. It came about after months of trying to master a simple white sour (our classic loaf). I had sorted out the basics, but was tired of the lack of variety from all this testing. As with most keen bakers, my cupboard was full of half-empty packets of flours and grains. And so, in an attempt to test my new-found bread skills, and spring clean the baking cupboard while I was at it, the country loaf was born. I mention how important it is not to change your brand/style of flour while getting to grips with dough, and in particular sourdough. This recipe, however, is brilliant to play around with once you feel you have gotten the hang of things and want to move onto the next step. The quantities of the various flours in the recipe are so small that it shouldn't disrupt the consistency too much when substituted for others. That said, if you play around with the rye and spelt levels, take note of how much wetter or stiffer the dough becomes. Don't be afraid to play with the water quantity at the same time – now you are at this stage, it's good to go with your gut and achieve a consistency that feels familiar as opposed to an exact measurement. It's a great way to start getting a feel for the alternatives to your classic strong white bread flour.

Makes 1 loaf

200 g (7 oz/¾ cup) water
75 g (2½ oz) Active starter (see page 26)
150 g (5¼ oz/1¼ cups) strong white bread flour
100 g (3½ oz/¾ cup) granary flour
30 g (2 tablespoons) rye flour
30 g (2 tablespoons) spelt flour
10 g (2 teaspoons) salt

The method and baking time is the same as for the Classic sourdough on page 28.

PORRIDGE

A beautiful loaf that contains a high percentage of water in comparison to most of our loaves. This is due to the absorbency of oats, which means you can sneak in a lot more liquid than you would normally expect. This is the best loaf for toasting because of its creamy and soft texture.

Makes 1 loaf

60 g (2¼ oz/¾ cup) rolled oats, plus extra for topping
60 g (2¼ oz/¼ cup) boiling water
150 g (5¼ oz/⅔ cup) hand-warm water
75 g (2½ oz) Active starter (see page 26)
250 g (8¾ oz/2 cups) strong white bread flour
10 g (2 teaspoons) salt

Add the oats and boiling water to a freestanding mixer or bowl. Mix until combined and allow to cool. Once cooled, add the remaining ingredients and mix either with a dough hook or by hand, kneading as instructed in the Classic sourdough recipe (see page 28).

Remove from the mixer and place in a lightly oiled bowl. Prove for 2 hours.

Roll the proved dough into a tight ball and let prove on the work surface for a further 5 minutes to allow the dough to relax before its final shaping.

Shape as instructed in the Classic sourdough recipe (see page 28). Dip the whole loaf in a bowl of warm water and then quickly dip it into a waiting bowl of oats to completely cover the loaf. Place seam-side up in a cloth-lined basket. Prove for a further 2 hours, then place in the refrigerator overnight.

The next day, follow the same baking instructions as on page 28.

SESAME AND SPELT

This loaf has a slightly tighter crumb due to the characteristics of spelt flour, but it is just as delicious due to the nutty and wholesome flavour that spelt provides.

Makes 1 loaf

160 g (5½ oz/1⅓ cups) strong white bread flour
160 g (5½ oz/1⅓ cups) spelt flour
10 g (2 teaspoons) salt
75 g (2½ oz) Active starter (see page 26)
200 g (7 oz/¾ cup) water
15 g (1 tablespoon) white sesame seeds, plus extra for topping
15 g (1 tablespoon) black sesame seeds, plus extra for topping

Combine all the ingredients together and follow the instructions for proving and shaping as for Classic sourdough (see page 28).

Just before you are about to place your bread in the oven, tip the loaf from its basket and brush the top with water. Sprinkle generously with a mixture of white and black sesame seeds. Slash down the middle with your knife at an angle.

Bake as usual (see page 28).

RYE

This recipe exists solely because of Justin Tunstall's amazing knowledge of dough. I spent a long time playing with 100 per cent rye loaves, and frankly didn't have much joy with them. When Justin joined the bakery last year, I asked him to give it a go. I had become a bit despondent about rye in general – it can be a cruel mistress. Only two trials later, he produced this method and baked a batch of these lovely little loaves. In the shop we wrap them in greaseproof paper so they look like small gifts. In my opinion, they really are a gift.

Makes 2 x 450 g (1 lb) loaves

for the rye starter
130 g (4½ oz) Active starter (see page 26)
260 g (9 oz/1 generous cup) water
200 g (7 oz/1⅔ cups) light rye flour,
    plus extra for dusting

for the dough
330 g (11½ oz/1¾ cups) dark rye flour
15 g (1 tablespoon) salt
250 g (8¾ oz/1 cup) water
15 g (1 tablespoon) treacle
15 g (1 tablespoon) sunflower seeds
15 g (1 tablespoon) linseeds

First, make the rye starter. Mix the starter, water and light rye flour together in a large bowl. Cover with cling film (plastic wrap) and allow to prove for 2–3 hours. You should notice a growth in size. Try not to leave it for too much longer, as you risk the flavour becoming too sour.

Add the remaining ingredients to the rye starter. You only want to mix this until everything is combined. You don't require any gluten development for this recipe, so it doesn't need to be worked above and beyond. Re-cover the bowl and prove the dough for 2 hours. Once noticeably grown in size, scrape the dough out onto a wet or oiled work surface. The water or oil will help prevent the dough from sticking. With wet hands, split the dough in half. Place your two lots of dough directly into two greased 450 g (1 lb) loaf tins. You don't need to faff around trying to shape this dough too much as you will find it is quite wet and tricky to handle. Prove in the tins for 1 hour, then transfer to the refrigerator in order to prove slowly overnight.

The next morning, remove the dough from the refrigerator and allow to come to room temperature, about 30 minutes. Sprinkle the tops of the loaves with a little light rye flour. Bake at 230ºC (450ºF/Gas 9) for 50 minutes–1 hour. If you notice the tops colouring too much, cover loosely with foil. It requires a long bake because of how sticky the dough is. It is cooked when it is a deep dark brown and the flour on top has 'cracked'.

Allow to cool completely before slicing. The loaves will keep really well for 3–5 days.

FIG AND FENNEL

A sweeter loaf that was born to be topped with a big hunk of brie or Chaource cheese. It is important to soak the fruit the night before in order to soften the figs and prevent them from burning or drying out when baked.

Makes 1 loaf

260 g (9 oz/2¼ cups) strong white bread flour
10 g (2 teaspoons) salt
80 g (2½ oz) Active starter (see page 26)
100 g (3½ oz/scant ½ cup) water

for the fig and fennel soak
90 g (3 oz/⅔ cup) dried figs, chopped
15 g (1 tablespoon) fennel seeds
60 g (2 oz/¼ cup) boiling water

Weigh out all of the soaking ingredients in a bowl. Cover with cling film (plastic wrap) and leave overnight, or for at least 6 hours. This helps to soften the figs.

The next day, combine the soaked ingredients, including any remaining water, with the rest of the ingredients. Follow the instructions and method for Classic sourdough (see page 28); the baking time also remains the same.

TURMERIC AND SHALLOT

A 'Scott Special', as we like to call it in the bakery. When Scott is left to his own devices in the bread room, it's unusual for a batch of this dough not to be mixed up. As tasty as it is vibrant in colour.

Makes 1 loaf

olive oil, for frying
75 g (2½ oz/⅓ cup) shallots, finely sliced
1 teaspoon ground turmeric
275 g (9¾ oz/2¼ cups) strong white bread flour
10 g (2 teaspoons) salt
150 g (5¼ oz/⅔ cup) water
90 g (3 oz) Active starter (see page 26)

Heat a large frying pan (skillet) with a little oil over a medium heat. Cook the shallots until softened and just beginning to caramelise, around 5–8 minutes. Set aside to cool completely.

Combine all the ingredients together and follow the instructions and method for Classic sourdough (see page 28).

OVERNIGHT BAGUETTES

Sourdough provides an amazing quality to baguettes. The result is an ultra-crisp crust (the skin that forms when left overnight helps this, as well as a clean cut) and a lovely open crumb and interior. Serve with soft cheese and cured meats and – ta-dah! – you are in the Alps.

Makes 3 large baguettes

2 quantities of Classic sourdough (see page 28)
olive oil, for oiling
extra flour, for dusting
semolina, for dusting

Follow the sourdough method on page 28 up until the end of its first prove. Tip the dough back onto a lightly oiled work surface. Divide into 6 equal pieces, weighing 400 g (14 oz) each. Shape into rounds. The easiest way to do this is to cup both hands then use them to tuck both sides of the dough underneath until your pinkies meet. Rotate 90 degrees and repeat until you have a tight ball. Allow to rest on the work surface for 10 minutes. This relaxes the dough and makes it easier to form your final shape.

Once the doughs have relaxed, sprinkle your work surface and one of the pieces of dough with more flour. Gently but firmly pat the dough into a rough rectangle shape. Make sure the bottom isn't sticking to the work surface. Fold over the top third of the dough and use the heel of your hands and thumbs to seal the edge. Fold the bottom third of the dough up and use the heel of your hands and thumbs to seal the edge. Flip the dough over. Start with both hands in the middle of the dough and roll them back and forth over the top of the dough gently until you reach either end. Repeat until you have the desired length you want. Use the heel of your hands to form a sharp tip at either end. Transfer the shaped baguette to a baking tray lined with a big piece of lightly floured linen cloth (a couche) or a lightly floured tea towel. Create a ridge in the fabric so you can place the next baguette alongside without it sticking.

Repeat for the rest of the dough. Cover the baguettes with any excess fabric or another tea towel and set aside at room temperature for 2 hours. Cling film (plastic wrap) the tray and place in the refrigerator overnight. You can bake them immediately; however, we like the flavour that develops when they are left overnight. The dough is also much easier to score when it has firmed up a bit after chilling.

About 30 minutes before baking, remove the baguettes from the refrigerator to bring back to room temperature. Preheat your oven to 230ºC (450ºF/Gas 9). Place a baking stone or heavy-duty baking (cookie) sheet in the oven to preheat at the same time.

Once the oven is hot and the dough has warmed up, you are ready to bake. Dust the top of the baguettes with a little semolina. Carefully remove the hot stone or sheet from the oven. Gently tip one baguette onto the hot surface and, working quickly, score a few slashes down the middle of the stick, with your knife at a 45-degree angle. We use a serrated knife for the job. Chuck a handful of ice cubes onto the base of the oven, then return the stone or sheet to the oven. Close the door quickly to stop any steam escaping. Bake for 15–20 minutes before opening the door to allow the steam out. Bake for a further 5–10 minutes until dark in colour and hollow-sounding when tapped. Best eaten still warm.

FOCACCIA

Ninety per cent hydration means this dough is wild and wet. This helps to contribute to a damp, soft, open crumb that is bouncy in texture. Wetter is always better for focaccia, so it is worth taking your time when it comes to kneading this dough. You want to build up the gluten as much as possible to form a brilliantly elastic dough – the result will be all the chewier for it. You can keep it simple with just a scattering of sea salt flakes, but we like to vary it; our favourite toppings are caramelised red onion and black sesame seed (see picture opposite), artichoke and sage, sunblushed tomato and thyme, and rosemary and sea salt (see picture overleaf).

Makes 1 loaf

500 g (1 lb 1½ oz/4 cups) strong white bread flour
450 g (1 lb/1¾ cups) water
10 g (2 teaspoons) salt
7 g (1 generous teaspoon) dried instant action yeast
25 g (1½ tablespoons) extra virgin olive oil, plus extra for the tin and to serve
sea salt flakes, for topping

Weigh out all of the ingredients, but only 400 g (14 oz/1⅔ cups) of the water into the bowl of a free-standing mixer. This recipe is best done in a mixer, if you have one, as the dough it quite wet and difficult to knead by hand. Mix on slow speed for 4 minutes, then turn the mixer up and mix on high speed for 6 minutes. Let the dough sit in the mixer for 15 minutes, to rest, or autolyse, if you are being technical. Restart the mixer and add the remaining water. Mix for a further 4 minutes on a slow speed. Remove the dough from the mixer and prove for 1 hour, giving intermediate folds every 15 minutes. For folding techniques look at the method for the Classic sourdough (see page 28). Transfer to a plastic container or Tupperware and store in the refrigerator overnight.

In the morning, tip the dough into a lightly oiled 20 x 30 cm (8 x 12 in) roasting tin, and with wet hands stretch out to fit the tin. Leave for 2 hours, giving the dough a stretch every 30 minutes.

Half an hour before the dough is ready, preheat the oven to 230ºC (450ºF/Gas 9). Add any toppings you fancy and sprinkle the top with salt flakes. Bake for 15–20 minutes, or until cooked through and golden on the bottom. Drizzle with extra virgin olive oil and serve.

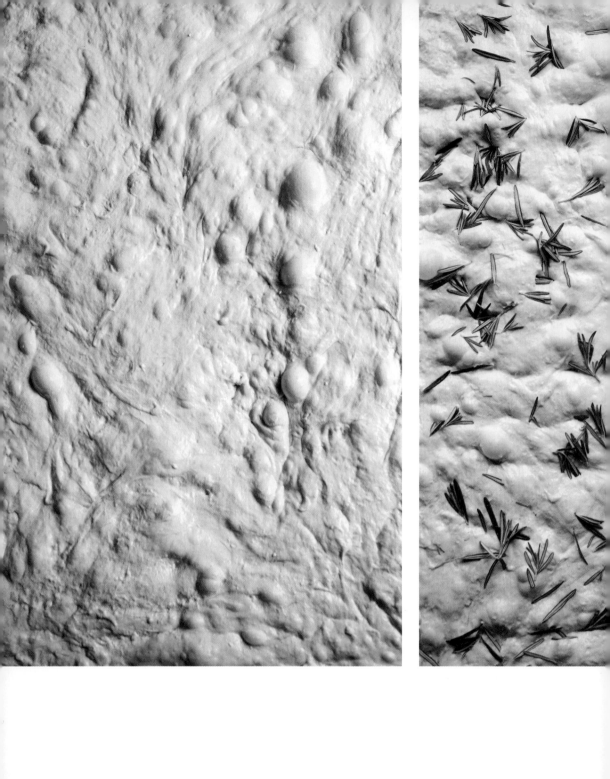

Rosemary and sea salt focaccia

2. THE WEE HOURS

As the birds sing

Once the sun begins its slow struggle upwards and the birds start to twitter; once our ovens are up and running and our bread scored and fired; we set about our pastries and our laminated doughs. The doughs that take a little sweetness and a lot of time. The creations best eaten straight after baking and never ever the next day. The recipes that require attention, but give nothing but rewards in return...

BRIOCHE

This is a wonderfully versatile dough and has been on our menu since day one. It is hugely popular when turned into buns (see pages 58 and 60) though arguably most things are when stuffed with custard.

Makes 1 loaf

500 g (1 lb 1½ oz/4 cups) plain (all-purpose) flour
125 g (4½ oz/⅔ cup) caster (superfine) sugar
100 g (4¼ fl oz/scant ½ cup) whole (full-fat) milk
100 g (4¼ fl oz/scant ½ cup) water
1 large egg, plus extra egg, beaten, for egg wash
10 g (⅓ oz/2 teaspoons) dried instant action yeast
250 g (8¾ oz) unsalted butter, softened

Weigh out all of the ingredients together in a free-standing mixer, being careful that the sugar and yeast don't touch at this stage. Beat using a dough hook (or by hand) until smooth and well combined. The butter should be soft before using, otherwise you will notice lumps throughout the mixture. If this happens, allow it to soften up, then mix again to fully incorporate.

We normally mix up this dough at the end of our working day and sit it in a cool spot to prove overnight. We are using the dough quite early, so if you want to bake at a leisurely pace, I would recommend popping it in the refrigerator. Either that or set an alarm for the crack of dawn… If you want to make your brioche in one day, the dough should be fully proved and ready to shape after 2 hours.

To shape the brioche into loaves, simply grease and line 2 large loaf tins, then split the dough in half to roughly the same length as each tin. They should be smooth and rounded when placed into the tins. Cover and leave to prove for another 2 hours, or until well risen and doubled in size.

Half an hour before they are finished proving, preheat the oven to 170ºC (340ºF/Gas 5). Lightly brush the loaves with egg wash, then slash down the middle with a knife at a 45-degree angle. Bake for 30–40 minutes, or until golden brown and glossy on top. Allow to cool for 20 minutes in the tin before turning out and cooling completely.

PEACH, CHOCOLATE AND ALMOND

Makes 12 buns

1 quantity of Brioche dough (see page 57)
extra flour, for dusting
1 egg, beaten
1 quantity of Crème pât (see page 228)
150 g (5¼ oz) dark chocolate, chopped
3-4 large white peaches
100 g (3½ oz) flaked (slivered) almonds
icing (confectioner's) sugar, for dusting

Follow the instructions to make the brioche dough and allow to prove for 2 hours.

Knock the dough back on a lightly floured surface. Divide into 12 equal balls, roughly 100 g (3½ oz) each. Gently shape each ball into a smooth round and dip the bottom in a little flour. Place each one into a small shallow tin, 10 cm (4 in) in diameter – ideally, one with a flat edge, but a fluted-edged tin will also work. You can do this free form, but the tins do help with a little bit of structure. Allow to prove for 30 minutes–1 hour until doubled in size.

Preheat the oven to 170°C (340°F/Gas 5).

Once doubled in size, use 2 fingers to gently press down the middle, forming a little bowl shape, making sure you leave a generous enough border, roughly 2–3 cm (1–1½ in) wide. Brush generously with egg wash. Spoon or pipe in a decent amount of crème pât into each bowl. Sprinkle the tops with chocolate, focusing on the border but also a little covering the crème pât. Quarter your peaches and cut each quarter into about 6 thin slices (see recipe picture opposite). Keeping them close together, fan the slices out like feathers. Carefully place each fanned quarter on top of the crème pât and sprinkle the bottom of the fruit with some flaked almonds.

Bake for 20 minutes, until golden brown and cooked through. The dough might look a little soft still, but you don't want to overcook it as it will become dry. Allow to cool in the tins for 15–20 minutes before removing. Dust with icing sugar to serve.

BLUEBERRY CRUMBLE

Makes 12 buns

1 quantity of Brioche dough (see page 57)
extra flour, for dusting
1 egg, beaten
1 quantity of Crème pât (see page 228)
1 quantity of Oat crumble (see page 227)
200 g (7 oz) blueberries
icing (confectioner's) sugar, for dusting

Follow the instructions to make the brioche dough and allow to prove for 2 hours.

Knock the dough back on a lightly floured surface. Divide into 12 equal balls, of roughly 100 g (3½ oz) each. Gently shape each ball into a smooth round and dip the bottom in a little flour. Place each one into a small shallow tin, 10 cm (4 in) in diameter – ideally, one with a flat edge, but a fluted-edged tin will also work. You can do this free form, but the tins do help with a little bit of structure. Allow to prove for 30 minutes–1 hour until doubled in size.

Preheat the oven to 170ºC (340ºF/Gas 5).

Once doubled in size, use 2 fingers to gently press down the middle, forming a little bowl shape, making sure you leave a generous enough border, roughly 2–3 cm (1–1½ in) wide. Brush generously with egg wash. Spoon or pipe a decent amount of crème pât into each bowl. Sprinkle the tops with crumble, focusing on the border but also a little covering the crème pât. Stick a small handful of blueberries on top of the custard, making sure they won't go onto the border or fall out.

Bake for 20 minutes until golden brown and cooked through. The dough might look a little soft still, but you don't want to overcook it as it will become dry. Allow to cool in the tins for 15–20 minutes before removing. Dust with icing sugar to serve.

A NOTE ON CROISSANT LAYERS

TIME

On the face of it, three days seems like a massive time investment for a pastry. I understand this could be off-putting; however, once you have committed the time and energy, you won't go back. It is one of the most addictive processes and over the development of this recipe (we have tried more than 50 variations in my endless quest for 'LAYERZ') I have dedicated many three-day stints to finding out if that small tweak was going to make a difference or not. The recipe on page 67 has been developed to fit with your lifestyle (as well as ours) so, although it looks as though this is a large period of time, it is actually fairly simply to fit in around your day-to-day activities. As long as you are able to be around for the afternoon of the second day, you can come and go back to the dough in between other things.

WEATHER

If this is your first time baking croissants, you want the weather to be on your side. When we first opened the bakery, Scott and I used to wrestle with melting layers in the heat of the kitchen, regularly offering the job to each other in order to get out of the lamination race. How the French invented croissants in such a warm climate is beyond me. The experience is altogether more enjoyable when you work in a cool environment and are afforded the luxury of time to roll out the dough and laminate carefully. Aim to work with the dough in an environment no warmer than 18ºC (65ºF), although ideally 14–15ºC (57–59ºF). This way, you will have more time for the whole process and less chance of your precious butter being absorbed by the dough. The crucial aim is to keep the butter solid between the layers of dough and, of course, the best way to do this is to keep the whole process as cool as possible.

PATIENCE

This is crucial. You must be patient and calm during the process. If you are getting frustrated (me, more often than not) or trying to rush things, your croissants will go wrong. Take your time, take a breath and follow the instructions carefully. The buttery deliciousness of these chaps will be all the sweeter because of it.

MAI

Mai, 3, is our youngest critic and croissant connoisseur.
She often arrives on the back of her dad's bike and we are
regularly greeted with a smile no one could refuse. A croissant
is one of her favourites choices, and we are always impressed
by her ability to polish off the whole thing in a short sitting.
Once finished, she spends the rest of her time in the bakery
making pals and drawing or reading. Apparently, my drawings
of croissants look a bit like sausages, and clearly don't have
a patch on her sketches.

What is your favourite thing to eat in the bakery?
EVERYTHING!

Why?
Because everything is very yummy!

How many layers do you think are in our croissants?
Maybe seven?

What do you like the most about the bakery?
The people are nice. They let me read their books.

Pear, hazelnut + coffee cake

Blueberry & custard brioche

Pistachio Loaf (GF)

Iced Gingerbread

Apple + cinnamon crumble

CROISSANTS

This recipe is dedicated to all the bakers that have put up with my endless tweaks, method changes, recipe alterations and not always successful intel I have discovered on the various croissant forums I have now become an avid reader of. Although I probably can't help myself when it comes to alterations I genuinely think we have finally sussed it, guys! Thank you for your eternal patience. See page 62 for everything you need to know before you begin.

Makes 8

for the dough
500 g (1 lb 1½ oz/4 cups) strong white
    bread flour, plus extra for dusting
75 g (2½ oz/⅓ cup) caster (superfine) sugar
25 g (1½ tablespoons) melted butter
7 g (1 teaspoon) dried instant action yeast
150 g (5¼ oz/⅓ cup) whole (full-fat) milk

150 g (5¼ oz/⅓ cup) water
5 g (scant 1 teaspoon) salt

for the lamination and glazing
250 g (8¾ oz) unsalted butter,
    refrigerator cold
extra flour, for dusting
1 egg, beaten

DAY ONE *evening*

Combine all the dough ingredients and knead for 10 minutes by hand or for 3–4 minutes in the bowl of a free-standing mixer at low to medium speed. The dough should come together and reach a stage of low to moderate gluten development. You are not looking for a huge amount of elasticity, but you should notice the dough is soft and springy. Unlike with breadmaking, you do not want too much gluten development because you will struggle with the dough fighting back during laminating. Flatten the dough into a rough rectangle and cover with cling film (plastic wrap). Transfer to a baking (cookie) sheet and chill in the refrigerator overnight. This makes it easier for you to roll out the following day.

DAY TWO *midday*

Cut the refrigerator-cold butter for laminating lengthways into four equally thick slabs. Arrange the pieces of butter on greaseproof paper, then cover with another layer of greaseproof paper. Use a rolling pin to pound the butter until it is 5 mm (¼ in) thick and roughly 20 cm (8 in) square. Straighten the edges of the butter and press any excess back into the square. Wrap in cling film, then refrigerate until needed. You want to chill it for at least 1 hour.

Continued overleaf

DAY TWO *afternoon*

Take the dough out of the refrigerator and place on a very lightly floured work surface. With a rolling pin, roll out the dough to roughly 30 cm (12 in) square. Try to get the square as even as possible in terms of thickness. If you make sure your thickness is always consistent, your layers will be consistent also. Get the slab of butter from the refrigerator and place it in middle of the dough at a 45-degree angle. You should have 4 equal triangles of dough still exposed with the butter covering the middle. Fold each triangle of dough over the butter, so the points of the triangle meet in the middle. The edges of the dough flaps should slightly overlap to fully enclose the butter. With the palm of your hand, lightly press the edges to seal the seams, but make sure you don't press too hard and damage the first layer.

With a lightly floured rolling pin, start rolling out the dough to a rectangle of 20 x 60 cm (8 x 24 in). Do this gently and gradually, starting from the middle of the dough and working out towards the edges. This helps ensure an even thickness. Make sure you always roll away from yourself, moving the dough when required as opposed to the rolling pin. Rolling in one direction only also helps with consistency. You want to lengthen the dough rather than make it wider and try to keep all the edges as straight as possible. Don't use too much flour on the work surface as this can make the layers of the dough tough and ruin the overall effect. If your dough remains cold enough, you shouldn't have too many issues with it sticking. Brush off any excess flour with a dry pastry brush.

Fold the top of the dough over itself, by roughly 5 cm (2 in). Fold the bottom half of the dough up on itself so that the seams meet. You should end up with a seam near the top of the dough and a rectangle that is now 20 cm (8 in) wide and 30 cm (12 in) tall. Fold the dough in half to form a rectangle 20 cm (8 in) wide and 15 cm (6 in) tall. This is called a book fold. Cover in cling film and chill for 30 minutes–1 hour. The trick here is to keep the butter cold enough so it doesn't get absorbed into the dough, but warm enough that it can be rolled. If you find the butter cracks and splits when you roll it out, it has been chilled for too long. Leave at room temperature for 15 minutes, then try again. You want the butter to stay as one thin, continuous layer.

Repeat the rolling and folding one more time, following the above instructions. Make sure you turn the dough 90 degrees before rolling again. The open 'end' of the dough (i.e. where you would open the book) should be on the right-hand side if your dough is vertically in front of you after the turn. After the second fold, allow the dough to rest for another hour in the refrigerator.

It is worth noting that sometimes the dough will resist any more rolling before you reach 60 cm (24 in). If this happens, stop rolling, cover the dough and let it relax for 10–20 minutes in the refrigerator before continuing. If it is fighting you, don't fight back, as you risk damaging the layers. Patience is key.

Continued overleaf

DAY TWO *evening*

Take the dough from the refrigerator and return to your lightly floured work surface. Very gently roll the dough into a long rectangle of 30 x 50 cm (12 x 20 in). If the dough starts to resist too much or shrink back during this process, gently fold it in half and allow the gluten to relax for 10–20 minutes in the refrigerator again.

When your dough has reached the right size, gently lift to make sure it hasn't stuck and allow for any natural spring back. Your strip of dough should be long enough to allow you to trim the ends to make them straight and still be left with a length of about 45 cm (18 in) and 5 mm (¼ in) thick. Your dough should be roughly 25 cm (10 in) wide.

Using a ruler, measure and make a small notch every 10 cm (4 in) along one long edge of the dough, working from left to right. On the opposite long edge, measure 5 cm (2 in) in from the left-hand edge of the dough, then repeat the process of making a notch every 10 cm (4 in). The top notches should be exactly half way between the bottom ones. Cut triangles starting from the first top notch cutting down to the first bottom notch, then from the same top notch cutting down to the second bottom notch. Repeat this along the length of the dough. You should end up with at least 8 croissants, though sometimes you can sneak an extra one on the end, depending on how wide you managed to roll the dough.

Now very gently elongate each triangle to about 30 cm (12 in) using your hands to slowly tease it out. If the dough doesn't want to stretch, stop and allow it to rest for 5 minutes on the work surface, then try again.

Roll the dough upwards, starting from the wide base of the triangle. Do this tightly at the beginning and put enough pressure on the dough to make the layers stick together, but not so much as to damage the layers, of course. Twist the tip of the dough and press it underneath the croissant.

Arrange the shaped croissants on baking sheets (that aren't too big to fit inside your refrigerator), making sure to keep enough space between them so they will not touch when proving and baking. Give the croissants a thin coating of egg wash, then reserve the egg for a second coat.

Place the croissants in the refrigerator overnight.

DAY THREE *morning*

The morning of baking, you need to bring the croissants out to prove. We prove our croissants in our fan ovens, preheated to 25°C (77°F) for 10–15 minutes then turned off. Make sure the oven door is closed while proving. They will take 30 minutes–1 hour at this temperature, but keep an eye on them in case your oven is extra efficient. You can of course prove them at room temperature; however, if you are in a colder climate, as we are in Scotland, this can take as long as 3 hours. If they aren't quite ready in time, don't be afraid to prove them for longer – it would be heartbreaking to bake them under-proved after all this work. You'll be able to tell if they are ready by carefully shaking the baking sheet; the croissants will slightly jiggle, much like a just-set custard. You should also be able to see the layers of dough beginning to separate when looking at your croissants from the side.

Remove the croissants from the oven if using it to prove and preheat the oven to 170°C (340°F/Gas 5).

Just before baking, give the croissants their second coat of egg wash. Place in the preheated oven and bake for 20–30 minutes or until evenly golden brown. Remove from the oven, let sit for a few minutes on the baking sheet, then transfer to a cooling rack.

If your croissants have leaked a large quantity of butter, this is a tell-tale sign that they were under-proved before baking. Bear this in mind for future bakes.

They are, of course, best eaten while warm and fresh; croissants we don't eat within a day are used to make almond croissants the next day (see page 73). They also make excellent bread and butter pudding laden with chocolate and hazelnuts.

TWICE-BAKED ALMOND

We initially planned on making these with the leftover croissants that we assumed we would have. When it became clear that leftovers were going to be rarity at Aran, we started baking an extra load of croissants the day before so we could make almonds ones, too. They are totally indulgent, wildly popular and well worth the sin of allowing a croissant to go stale.

Makes 12

12 stale croissants
1 batch of Frangipane (see page 227)
flaked (slivered) almonds, to decorate
icing (confectioner's) sugar, to dust

for the syrup
500 g (1 lb 1½ oz/2 cups) water
500 g (1 lb 1½ oz/2½ cups) caster
  (superfine) sugar
1 teaspoon vanilla bean paste
100 g (3½ oz/scant ½ cup) brandy
  or amaretto (optional)

Preheat the oven to 160°C (320°F/Gas 4). Grease and line 2 baking (cookie) sheets.

Begin with the syrup. Place all the ingredients except for the alcohol in a pan and bring to the boil over a medium heat. Once the sugar has completely dissolved, remove from the heat and add the alcohol, if using. Stir well, then set aside to cool down completely.

Make the frangipane and transfer to a piping (pastry) bag fitted with a plain nozzle.

Cut the croissants in half lengthways. Dunk them in the sugar syrup for a few seconds, then squeeze lightly to get rid of any excess syrup. Arrange your soaked croissant halves on the prepared baking sheets. Pipe a couple of lines or a zigzag of frangipane into the middle of each croissant then stick the lid on top. Pipe a line down the length of the top of the croissant and use to stick flaked almonds to the top. Repeat with the other croissants. Once ready, place in the oven for 20–30 minutes or until golden and the frangipane has just set. Dust with icing sugar and enjoy warm and on the same day as baking.

PAC

The classic pain au chocolat. You are lying if you say you don't eat the chocolaty middle first.

Makes 9

1 quantity of Croissant dough, after its final book fold (see pages 67-69)
extra flour, for dusting
approx. 100 g (3½ oz) 54% chocolate batons, or dark chocolate roughly chopped into sticks
1 egg, for glazing

Take the dough from the refrigerator and place on a lightly floured work surface. Very gently roll the dough into a long rectangle of 30 x 50 cm (12 x 20 in). If the dough starts to resist too much or shrink back during this process, gently fold it in half and allow the dough to relax for 10–20 minutes in the refrigerator again.

When your dough has reached the right size, gently lift to make sure it hasn't stuck and allow for any natural spring back. Your strip of dough should be long enough to allow you to trim the ends to make them straight and still be left with a length of about 45 cm (18 in) and 5 mm (¼ in) thick. Your dough should be roughly 25 cm (10 in) wide.

Using a ruler, measure and make a small notch every 15 cm (6 in) along the bottom longer length of the dough. On the left-hand shorter edge of the dough, make a small notch every 8 cm (3 in). Horizontally cut 3 long strips of dough where you have marked the 8 cm (3 in) notches. Use the marks at the bottom to cut each long strip into 3 lengths of 15 cm (6 in) each. You should have 9 rectangles, each measuring 8 x 15 cm (3 x 6 in).

Place a stick of chocolate along one of the 8 cm (3 in) edges. Roll the dough over the stick to cover it. Place a second stick next to the dough where it has been folded over, then continue to roll until you reach the end of the rectangle. Arrange each pastry on a baking (cookie) sheet lined with greaseproof paper, seam-side down. Egg wash the top generously, then allow to prove as below, or place in the refrigerator overnight until ready to bake.

We prove our PAC in our fan ovens, preheated to 25°C (77°F) for 10–15 minutes then turned off. Make sure the oven door is closed while proving. They will take 30 minutes–1 hour at this temperature, but keep an eye on them in case your oven is extra efficient. You can of course prove them at room temperature; however, if you are in a colder climate, as we are in Scotland, this can take as long as 3 hours. If they aren't quite ready, don't be afraid to prove them for longer – it would be heartbreaking to bake them under-proved after all this work. You can tell if they are ready by carefully shaking the baking sheet; the PAC should slightly jiggle, much like a just-set custard. You should also be able to see the layers of dough beginning to separate when looking at your PAC from the side. They should be doubled in size and pillow-like.

Remove the PAC from the oven if using it to prove and preheat the oven to 160ºC (320ºF/Gas 4).

Just before baking, give the PAC their second coat of egg wash. Place in the preheated oven and bake for 20–30 minutes or until evenly golden brown and oozing chocolate. Remove from the oven, let sit for a few minutes on the baking sheet, then transfer to a cooling rack. Enjoy warm, when you are likely to get chocolate all over your face. It is no fun otherwise.

RHUBARB PISTACHIO DANISH

I adore these little 'pink kites'. They are often complimented as they are a great shape for showing off all of the layers in the dough (see recipe picture overleaf). Well, that and because they are a really rather pretty shade of pink…

Makes 16

1 quantity of Croissant dough, after
    its final book fold (see pages 67–69)
extra flour, for dusting
1 egg, for glazing
½ quantity of Crème pât (see page 228)
about 40 g (1½ oz) pistachios, Iranian
    if you can get them for their vibrant
    green, blitzed
icing (confectioner's) sugar, for dusting

for the rhubarb
250 g (8¾ oz/1¼ cups) caster
    (superfine) sugar
1 teaspoon vanilla bean paste
1 orange, strips of peel only
250 g (8¾ oz/1 cup) water
400 g (14 oz) rhubarb, chopped
    into 5 cm (2 in) sticks

Start with the rhubarb. Mix the sugar, vanilla, orange rind and water in a saucepan and bring to the boil over a medium-high heat. Add the rhubarb to the boiling syrup, then immediately turn the heat down to medium-low. Simmer for 5 minutes then remove the pan from the heat. Allow the rhubarb to cool completely in the syrup. Decant the rhubarb and the syrup into an airtight tub and store in the refrigerator for up to 1 week. This recipe makes more than is required for the Danish pastries; however, it is delicious and makes for a perfectly pink treat! Serve with yoghurt for a colourful breakfast, or with ice cream and crushed ginger nut biscuits for a quick pudding.

For the pastries, take the dough from the refrigerator and place on a lightly floured work surface. Very gently roll the dough into a square, roughly 40 cm (16 in). If the dough starts to resist too much or shrink back during this process, gently fold it in half and allow it to relax for 10–20 minutes in the refrigerator again.

When your dough has reached the right size, gently lift to make sure it hasn't stuck and allow for any natural spring back. Your square dough should be big enough to allow you to trim the edges to make them straight and still be left with a square of about 36 cm (14 in) and 5 mm (¼ in) thick.

Using a ruler, measure and make a small notch every 9 cm (3½ cm) along the bottom and the left-hand edges of the dough. Horizontally cut 4 long strips of dough where you have marked the notches. Use the notches at the bottom to cut each long strip into 4 equal squares. You should have 16 squares.

To make the kite shape, gently fold the square in half diagonally. Make two diagonal cuts 1½ cm (½ in) from the outside edge. Make sure these diagonal cuts don't join at the tip of the triangle. Unfold the dough. Brush the whole surface with a little egg wash. Take the outer 'frame' edge and fold it over until it meets the cut you just made. Repeat on the other side, pulling it over the first edge to form a diamond shape. Do this on all of the squares.

Arrange the shaped pastries on 2 lined baking (cookie) sheets and brush the square 'ridge' with egg wash. Place the crème pât into a piping (pastry) bag and pipe into the central square of the pastry. Keep any excess crème pât as you can often fit more in once they have proved a little. Allow to prove immediately or place in the refrigerator overnight until ready to bake.

We prove our Danish pastries in our fan ovens, preheated to 25°C (77°F) for 10–15 minutes then turned off. Make sure the oven door is closed while proving. They will take 30 minutes–1 hour at this temperature, but keep an eye on them in case your oven is extra efficient. You can of course prove them at room temperature; however, if you are in a colder climate, as we are in Scotland, this can take as long as 3 hours. If they aren't quite ready, don't be afraid to prove them for longer – it would be heartbreaking to bake them under-proved after all this work. The Danishes should slightly jiggle, like a just-set custard, when you shake the baking sheet. You should also be able to see the layers of dough beginning to separate all around the edge of the Danish pastries. They should be doubled in size and the edges should look almost wing-like. Once proved, pipe any excess crème pât into the middle if there is space, but be careful not to overfill.

Remove the Danishes from the oven if using it to prove and preheat to 160°C (320°F/Gas 4).

Just before baking, give the pastries their second coat of egg wash. Place in the preheated oven and bake for 20–30 minutes or until evenly golden brown and the crème pât has sunk back on itself slightly. Remove from the oven, let sit for a few minutes on the baking sheet, then transfer to a cooling rack. Brush the edges with a little of the rhubarb syrup. Place the cooled rhubarb on top of the crème pât. Sprinkle one side of the pastries with pistachio nuts, then dust the other side with icing sugar. Enjoy warm with a cup of tea and a grin on your face.

*Rhubarb pistachio Danish (left) and
Pear tarragon Danish (right)*

PEAR TARRAGON DANISH

Tarragon crème pât was met with a fair few raised eyebrows when I first brought it up in the bakery; however, I remain adamant that it marries well with pear and enhances its natural sweetness (see recipe picture on page 78). Another good combo would be peach with a basil crème pât; however, I'm taking it one step at a time with the bakery boys...

Makes 16

1 quantity of Croissant dough,
    after its final book fold (see pages 67-69)
extra flour, for dusting
1 egg, for glazing
icing (confectioner's) sugar, to dust
tarragon to garnish

for the tarragon crème pât
250 g (8¾ oz/1 cup) whole (full-fat) milk
5 g tarragon, finely chopped
1 egg
15 g (1 tablespoon) cornflour (cornstarch)

40 g (1½ oz/3 tablespoons) caster
    (superfine) sugar
¼ teaspoon vanilla bean paste

for the poached pears
500 g (1 lb 1½ oz/2 cups) water
250 g (8¾ oz/1¼ cups) caster
    (superfine) sugar
1 vanilla pod, cut in half, or 1 teaspoon
    vanilla bean paste
1 lemon, thickly sliced
100 g (3½ oz/scant ½ cup) white wine
5 ripe pears

Begin with the poached pears. Place all the ingredients except the pears in a stainless steel saucepan. Peel the pears and place them directly into the pan to prevent browning. Place on a medium heat and bring to the boil. Once boiling, reduce the heat to maintain a simmer. Place a lid on the pan. The cooking time will depend on the ripeness of the pears. They are cooked when a fine knife is easily inserted into the middle of the fruit. Once cooked, remove the pan from the heat and allow the pears to cool in the sugar syrup. Allow to cool completely then transfer into an airtight container and store in the refrigerator for up to 1 week.

To make the crème pât, bring the milk and the tarragon to a simmer in a large saucepan. When it's almost boiling, remove from the heat and allow to stand for 15–20 minutes to infuse. Strain the milk and then continue with the recipe as stated on page 228. Allow to cool completely before using.

For the pastry, take the dough from the refrigerator and place on a lightly floured work surface. Very gently roll the dough into a square, roughly 40 cm (16 in). If the dough starts to resist too much or shrink back during this process, gently fold it in half and allow it to relax for 10–20 minutes in the refrigerator again.

When your dough has reached the right size, gently lift to make sure it hasn't stuck and allow for any natural spring back. Your square dough should be big enough to allow you to trim the edges to make them straight and still be left with a square of about 36 cm (14 in) and 5 mm (¼ in) thick.

Using a ruler, measure and make a small notch every 9 cm (3 in) along the bottom and the left-hand edges of the dough. Horizontally cut 4 long strips of dough where you have marked the notches. Use the notches at the bottom to cut each long strip into 4 equal squares. You should have 16 squares measuring 9 cm (3 in).

To make the kite shape, gently fold the square in half diagonally. Make two diagonal cuts 1½ cm (¼ in) in from the outside edge. Make sure these diagonal cuts don't join at the tip of the triangle. Unfold the dough and brush the whole surface with a little egg wash. Take the outer 'frame' edge and fold it over until it meets the cut you just made. Repeat on the other side, pulling it over the first edge to form a diamond shape. Do this on all of the squares.

Arrange the shaped pastries on 2 lined baking (cookie) sheets and brush the square 'ridge' with egg wash. Place the tarragon crème pât into a piping (pastry) bag and pipe into the central square of the pastry. Keep any excess crème pât as you can often fit more in once they have proved a little. Allow to prove immediately or place in the refrigerator overnight until ready to bake.

We prove our Danish pastries in our fan ovens, preheated to 25°C (77°F) for 10–15 minutes then turned off. Make sure the oven door is closed while proving. They will take 30 minutes–1 hour at this temperature, but keep an eye on them in case your oven is extra efficient. You can of course prove them at room temperature; however, if you are in a colder climate, as we are in Scotland, this can take as long as 3 hours. If they aren't quite ready don't be afraid to prove them for longer – it would be heartbreaking to bake them under-proved after all this work. You can tell if they are ready by carefully shaking the baking sheet; the Danishes will slightly jiggle, much like a just-set custard. You should also be able to see the layers of dough beginning to separate all around the edge of the Danish pastries. They should be doubled in size and the edges should look almost wing-like. Once proved, pipe any excess crème pât into the middle if there is space, but be careful to not overfill.

Remove the pastries from the oven if using it to prove and preheat the oven to 160°C (320°F/Gas 4). Just before baking, give the pastries their second coat of egg wash. Place in the preheated oven and bake for 20–30 minutes or until evenly golden brown and the crème pât has sunk back on itself slightly. Remove from the oven, let sit for a few minutes on the baking sheet, then transfer to a cooling rack. Brush the edges with a little of the poached pear syrup.

Cut the pears into quarters and remove the cores. Placing each quarter core-side down, cut about 7 very thin slices. Keeping them close together, fan the slices out like feathers. Carefully place the fanned pears on top of the crème pât. Dust one half of the pastries with icing sugar, then, once cooled, garnish with a sprig of fresh tarragon.

SEMLOR

A traditional Swedish bun that we began making out of sheer curiosity more than anything else. Soft and stuffed with a spiced almond filling, they became an instant hit. They also became a source of great entertainment to a Swedish couple who happened to stop by on their holiday in Scotland – it was the first day of serving them. I don't think they could believe it to be honest!

Makes 10

for the buns
200 g (7 oz/¾ cup) water, slightly warm
50 g (1¾ oz/¼ cup) whole (full-fat) milk
50 g (1¾ oz) butter, melted
500 g (1 lb 1½ oz/4 cups) strong
    white flour, plus extra for dusting
90 g (3 oz/scant ½ cup) caster
    (superfine) sugar
7 g (1 teaspoon) dried instant action yeast

2 eggs
10 g (2 teaspoons) salt
3 g (½ teaspoon) ground cardamom

for the filling
350 g (12½ oz) marzipan
1 quantity of Crème pât (see page 228)
350 g (12½ oz/scant 1½ cups) double
    (heavy) cream
1 egg, beaten, for glazing
icing (confectioner's) sugar, for dusting

In the bowl of a free-standing mixer weigh out all of the ingredients for the buns. Mix using a dough hook on a slow speed for 5–6 minutes. You can do this by hand, but be aware that the dough is quite sticky initially. Tip into a lightly oiled bowl and prove for 1 hour.

Once the dough has noticeably grown in size, tip it onto a lightly floured or oiled surface. Using a set of scales, divide the dough into 100 g (3½ oz) lumps and roll into balls. Arrange on a greased and lined baking (cookie) sheet and prove for a further 1 hour.

Meanwhile, preheat the oven to 200ºC (400ºF/Gas 7). Brush the egg wash generously over the buns. Bake for 10–15 minutes, until golden brown. Cover with a tea towel and then allow to cool completely – this will help prevent a crust from forming.

When the buns have cooled, cut a 'lid' off the buns – roughly 1½ cm (¾ in) from the top. I like to cut a triangle off the top, but you can also make a straight cut to form a round. Scoop out roughly one-third of the inside of the bun and place the crumbs in the bowl of a food processor. Add the marzipan and 350 g (12½ oz) of the crème pât to the food processor and blitz on high until you have a thick almond custard that is spoonable and smooth in consistency. Spoon the filling back into the buns, being careful not to get any on the outside of the bun.

Whip the double cream with the remaining crème pât until stiff and transfer into a piping (pastry) bag fitted with a fluted nozzle. I use a closed star nozzle. Pipe on top of the almond filling in a spiral. Put the 'lids' back on and dust with icing sugar.

3. SUNRISE
Wake up to this

The sun has broken through and the light becomes pale and ever-changing.
While baking, you can lower your head for a moment and when you look up
again the world looks blue and fresh. It is breakfast time. For those back
of house, it's time to retreat and start working their magic all over
again. For those front of house, it's show time. Doors open.

A NOTE ON TOAST

If I am truly honest with myself, the only reason I began playing with all things bread was for the end goal. Not the glorious loaf crackling as it is removed from the oven, crust dark in colour and insides creamy and tender. That part was fun, but the real pleasure comes the following day. More often than not, the morning after baking bread, I would wake up to a loaf half the size of its former glory, torn and battered slightly, because hot bread can be ripped, but it must never be sliced. It is at this point of the day that the real magic happens. Crust now softer and crumb beginning to stale, you can slice big slabs of it and toast, fry or scorch to your heart's content. Slathered in butter – if your toast isn't swimming in a pool of gold afterwards you are doing it wrong – you can top, garnish and adorn until the cows come home (ideally with more butter after you have consumed vats of the stuff with equal quantities of toast).

The classic for me is butter and sea salt; however, my sister Hebe takes it a step further, cracking black pepper over the salty bread. She does only spread a tenth of the butter she should on top of her toast, but we all have our flaws so I do let this slide occasionally. My other half, James, goes for Marmite, something I only fell in love with after making him dozens of breakfasts laced with the black nectar.

The endless possibilities are to me what makes toast so appealing. After primary school, we would come home to cinnamon toast (an exotic treat that we assumed only our mum knew how to make). At university, I would eat endless dinners of silky scrambled eggs on toast, occasionally pushing the boat out and roasting some old tomatoes from the back of the refrigerator that no one claimed ownership of. There was also fancy toast dotted throughout these days. A delicious brunch at Little Collins in Amsterdam featuring harissa-marinated feta, tenderstem broccoli (broccolini), avocado and loads of mizuna (see page 150); the sourdough, charousse, membrillo and Dunsyre blue I spent a small fortune on from I. J. Mellis when I moved to St. Andrews, and of course the toast that was drizzled with the world's most expensive chocolate sauce, which I bought by mistake, of course. During the quieter winter at the bakery, we offer a menu containing nothing but toast-related products. Toast will always be my staple diet, and more often than not my inspiration for bread.

For the sweeter-toothed, there are also the endless possibilities associated with jam. There is something deeply satisfying about spooning sugary gooseberries onto your toast eight months after you picked them, or enjoying sticky marmalade three months prior to the oranges getting good again. Jam is a particularly delicious way of beating the seasons, and toast in its own little way is a smug triumph over time, bringing bread back from the brink. Maybe it's these reviving qualities that make toast and jam such a perfect start to the day?

JAMS

This is a basic-but-effective method that can be translated to all the following recipes. When making any form of jam, you need to remember the four key ingredients...

FRUIT

Your fruit should be fresh and in season so the flavour is the best it can possibly be. You can use frozen fruits for these recipes, but you must make sure they have been frozen when the fruit is slightly underripe or just about ripe. Otherwise, you may have issues with the jam not setting. Use any overripe fruits for chutneys or compotes, where the setting point isn't as crucial. You should also be mindful of the different levels of pectin that each fruit contains naturally – apples and most orchard fruits tend to set quite quickly and with not too much sugar in comparison to strawberries and softer fruits.

CITRUS

In my opinion, all jams should contain some citrus. More often than not, I use lemons as a form of acid to help break down the fruit and counteract the sometimes-overwhelming sweetness of jam. A lot of fruit has a natural amount of acidity, which helps extract the natural pectin, but there is no harm in adding some more to help it along its way. Lemon tends to be the best addition for this, but by all means give grapefruit or lime a go as well.

SUGAR

Sugar is the most important element of jam and can make the difference between a really delicious preserve and a sickly sweet creation that tastes nothing like the original fruit. A huge volume of recipes call for equal parts sugar to jam, which is something I have never really agreed with. All of our recipes tend to work on three-quarters the amount of sugar compared to fruit, which we have found tends to be the lowest you can go for a guaranteed set and long shelf life. If you still find these recipes too sweet, by all means cut it down to half the amount of sugar to fruit; however, please note that this will decrease the length of time it will keep for. We use jam sugar for all of our recipes, but if you are having issues sourcing it, granulated sugar works fine. Just keep in mind that it may require a slightly longer cooking time in order for the natural pectin to work its magic.

PECTIN

This is a natural setting agent much like agar agar or gelatine. It tends to be found in most fruits, but the levels do vary. You can buy powdered pectin, but, much like agar agar, it is very tricky to get the quantities correct, so I much prefer relying on jam sugar (which has pectin already added) and the natural pectin in the fruit for my recipes.

Continued overleaf

Once you're comfortable with the ingredients and have chosen your fruit and flavours, you must make sure you carry out the sterilisation properly. It's boring and meticulous, but an essential part of the whole process. The last thing you want to do is spend hours preparing fruit and boiling your jam for the whole batch to spoil in a few weeks due to poor sterilisation.

Wash the jars and lids with hot soapy water, then place into a roasting tin and slide into an oven heated to 130ºC (260ºF/Gas 2) for about 15 minutes. Do the same with any utensils that will come into contact with the jam and jars once boiled; for example, we use a jam funnel and a small ladle to transfer the jam. Just before you start making the jam, pop some small plates into the freezer.

Start with the fruit and the citrus. Place in a large pan and bring to the boil, giving you a soft pulpy mixture. Add the sugar. Continue to heat, stirring all the time until the sugar has dissolved. Increase the heat to medium-high and bring the jam to a rolling boil. Cook for about 10 minutes.

To test if the jam is fully cooked, I always endorse the use of the 'wrinkle test'. Take one of the plates out of the freezer and spoon on a little of the jam. Pop the plate in the refrigerator for a couple minutes or so before pushing the jam with your finger. If it wrinkles and leaves a line where your finger has dragged through it will set, if it is still liquid and runny, cook it for a little longer. It is important to remember to always remove the jam from the heat while testing as you don't want it to overcook and become solid.

Once the jam has finished cooking, turn off the heat and leave for a minute or so to let it settle. If there is any foam on top carefully skim that off and discard (there is nothing wrong with the foam; however, as it is more aerated it can encourage the jam to spoil faster. Enjoy on toast to avoid wasting it). Remove the jars from the oven and carefully divide the jam between the warm jars. Cover the tops with greaseproof discs and seal. You can store the jars for up to a year, but once opened, they will keep in the refrigerator for up to 1 month.

We make all our own preserves and pickles at the bakery and also stock them on our shelves for sale. It never ceases to amaze me how much of the stuff we get through. When cooking at home, I would view a batch of jam or chutney as a day-long mission that would occur every three months or so as the season would change. Nowadays, we make kilos of the stuff on a weekly basis. Turns out everyone loves toast and jam as much as me.

GREENGAGE AND VANILLA

Makes approx. 8 x 300 g (10½ oz)
2 kg (4 lb 6½ oz) greengages
2 teaspoons vanilla bean paste
juice of 2 lemons
1.5 kg (3 lb 5 oz/12½ cups) jam sugar

STRAWBERRY, RHUBARB AND HIBISCUS

Makes approx. 8 x 300 g (10½ oz)
1 kg (2 lb 3¼ oz) strawberries
1 kg (2 lb 3¼ oz) rhubarb
5 hibiscus flowers
juice of 2 lemons
1.5 kg (3 lb 5 oz/12½ cups) jam sugar

GOOSEBERRY, PEAR AND ELDERFLOWER

Makes approx. 8 x 300 g (10½ oz)
1 kg (2 lb 3¼ oz) gooseberries, topped and tailed
1 kg (2 lb 3¼ oz) pears, peeled and chopped into rough chunks
juice of 2 lemons
1.5 kg (3 lb 5 oz/12½ cups) jam sugar
4 tablespoons elderflower cordial

Make sure you stir the cordial in at the end, once removed from the heat, to preserve the flavour. If you want, you can add some elderflowers in too, but again only add these at the end.

APPLE, BAY LEAF AND BRAMBLE

Makes approx. 8 x 300 g (10½ oz)
1 kg (2 lb 3¼ oz) apples, peeled and chopped into rough chunks
1 kg (2 lb 3¼ oz) brambles (blackberries)
5 bay leaves
juice of 2 lemons
1.5 kg (3 lb 5 oz/12½ cups) jam sugar

Make sure you remove the bay leaves before jarring. It is best to count them in and count them out.

BUTTERS

MARMITE BUTTER

For James, because we both find it near impossible to get the Marmite spread evenly.

150 g (5¼ oz) unsalted butter, softened
50 g (1¾ oz/¼ cup) Marmite
¼ teaspoon salt

Place the ingredients in a free-standing mixer fitted with the whisk attachment. Beat for 5 minutes or so until light, pale and fluffy. You can use a hand whisk, but this will take longer. Set aside at room temperature until ready to serve.

WHIPPED MAPLE BUTTER

The perfect accompaniment to pancakes, crumpets, toast, crêpes or any other carbohydrate crying out for a silky sweet topping.

150 g (5¼ oz) unsalted butter, softened
50 g (1¾ oz/¼ cup) maple syrup
1 teaspoon ground cinnamon

Place the ingredients in a free-standing mixer fitted with the whisk attachment. Beat for 5 minutes or so until light, pale and fluffy. You can use a hand whisk, but this will take longer. Set aside at room temperature until ready to serve.

ARAN GRANOLA

This is served daily as part of our breakfast menu at the shop. We dollop on thick yoghurt and top with seasonal fruit or whatever takes our fancy that week. I have been making variations of this recipe for more than seven years now and I have been thrilled by how popular it has been at the bakery. What is equally as thrilling is its simplicity and ability to be adapted and tweaked, as well as being scaled up. It is far more cost effective to make your own and also far more enjoyable – so long as the quantities remain roughly the same, you can tailor this to your taste, or what's in the cupboard.

Makes 1 large Kilner (Mason) jar

3 tablespoons coconut oil, melted, or any other light neutral-tasting oil
100 g (3½ oz/½ cup) maple syrup
100 g (3½ oz/½ cup) honey
1 teaspoon vanilla bean paste
350 g (12½ oz/4 cups) rolled oats
50 g (1¾ oz/¼ cup) sesame seeds
50 g (1¾ oz/¼ cup) poppy seeds
50 g (1¾ oz/¼ cup) pumpkin seeds
50 g (1¾ oz/¼ cup) flaked almonds
50 g (1¾ oz/¼ cup) hazelnuts, chopped
100 g (3½ oz/1 cup) coconut flakes

Preheat the oven to 140ºC (280ºF/Gas 3). In a large bowl, weigh out all the ingredients bar the coconut flakes. Mix together using your hands, making sure everything is well coated. Tip into a large roasting tin and place in the oven. Bake for 10 minutes before checking and stirring around the granola – this helps it to colour evenly. Bake for a further 10 minutes or until golden and becoming crisp. It will become crunchier once out of the oven too. Add the coconut flakes while still hot and mix through. Allow to cool completely before packing into a large jar or small cellophane gift bags.

POACHED QUINCE PORRIDGE

I first discovered quince in the brilliant Roots and Fruits in Glasgow. They aren't hugely available around our parts and seemed pretty 'exotic' to me back then. To be fair though, most things that you can't pick up from a low-level corner shop or highland supermarket normally get allocated to the 'exotic' category. A quince takes some fighting in order to make full use of its potential. A heavy kitchen knife is probably best, as well as a huge amount of caution. The peel has an infuriating habit of being glued to the fruit. It takes some tackling, but is well worth the effort.

The fruit is most commonly transformed almost miraculously into a dark red paste called membrillo. This only adds to its exoticness, as anything that can change colour so drastically is surely something to be marvelled at. It is tricky to make and often doesn't produce a huge amount in return, so I save membrillo for the rare and very special occasions when I have time on my hands.

This recipe makes more quince than is required for the porridge, but for the time and effort it is worth bulking up. Enjoy as a pudding with crème fraîche or on top of Aran granola (see page 97). It can also be mixed with custard and churned into a delicious ice cream.

Serves 2

250 g (8¾ oz/1 cup) water
150 g (5¼ oz/1⅔ cups) Scottish rolled oats,
    nothing else will do in my opinion…
250 g (8¾ oz/1 cup) milk, whole (full-fat)
    or almond work best
small pinch of salt
yoghurt, to serve

for the quince
750 g (1 lb 10½ oz/3 cups) water
150 g (5¼ oz/⅔ cup) caster
    (superfine) sugar
150 g (5¼ oz/scant ½ cup) honey
    or maple syrup
1 lemon, strips of rind only
1 vanilla pod, split lengthways or
    1 teaspoon vanilla bean paste
1 teaspoon ground ginger
5 large quince, peeled and cored

For the quince, heat the water with the sugar, honey, lemon and vanilla in a large saucepan. Bring to the boil.

While the liquid is on the heat, peel and core the quince. Make sure you remove everything tough and fibrous, as if not removed it can make your beautifully poached fruit quite tough. It will feel as though you are removing a huge amount of the core, but it is important that nothing firm or difficult to cut is left attached to the fruit. Slice into 1–2 cm (½ –1 in) wedges, and add them to the syrup as you are working. Much like apples and pears, quince tends to brown quite quickly once open to the air, so the sooner you get it in the syrup the better. Once they're all added to the liquid, cover the pan with a lid to prevent the syrup from reducing too much. Simmer the quince for roughly 1 hour, or until cooked through. You can tell this by piercing with a knife and seeing if it soft in consistency. Cooking time will vary, depending on the quince. Remove the fruit from the syrup and set aside to cool.

Sieve the lemon rinds and vanilla pod, if you have used one, out of the syrup. Crank up the heat and reduce the syrup by half or until it has thickened in consistency. Allow to cool a little, then return the fruit to the syrup. Store in an airtight container in the refrigerator for up to 1 week, making sure the fruit is always covered in the syrup.

For the porridge, place all the ingredients in a small pan and bring to the boil, stirring regularly. It should thicken within 3–4 minutes. Divide between 2 bowls. Top with yoghurt and the poached quince. Spoon over some of the syrup also. I like my porridge with a little more milk on top, but enjoy however you fancy.

SOUR CRUMPETS

This is based on a recipe by the wonderful Martha de Lacey, aka the sourdough queen of Instagram (@marthadelacey). It is a beautifully easy way to reuse any surplus starter if, like me, you hate to see it go to waste. During January, when we have our winter break and I am tasked with keeping Big Mumma, our starter, alive, I make these almost daily in order to prevent too much wastage.

Makes 6-8

75 g (2½ oz/⅓ cup) water
150 g (5¼ oz) Active starter (see page 26),
    or you can also use starved starter for this recipe
75 g (2½ oz/⅔ cup) plain (all-purpose) flour
1 teaspoon salt
1 tablespoon honey
1 teaspoon baking powder
butter, for frying and to serve
honey, to serve
Marmite, to serve

Whisk everything, except the butter, honey and Marmite, together to form a batter and set aside for 5 minutes to rest.

Heat a pan on the lowest setting with a little butter. Place 12 cm (6 in) metal rings into the pan and fill each half way up with batter. Allow to bubble up to the top (roughly 2–3 minutes), then cover with a pan lid to steam slightly. After about 2 minutes, remove the pan lid, then remove the ring (the crumpets should be pulling away from the sides and therefore easy to remove). Flip and cook for a further minute or so, then serve hot with an entire pack of butter and either Marmite or honey. I regularly choose both because the concept of committing to only one is quite stressful.

4. ELEVENSES
Mid-morning calm

The fluster of our morning delivery is through and we set about our process again,
looking ahead, tidying away the chaos of the early hours, planning those to come. Lunch
preparations begin, loaf cakes are mixed, the pace changes, cups of tea turn to coffee.

BLOOD ORANGE AND CARDAMOM/ LEMON AND POPPY SEED LOAF

Nothing quite beats citrus fruits when they are in their prime, so we have two versions of this cake to suit the seasonality. Blood oranges are incomparable at the start of the year, when you can make the most of them with this cardamom-spiked version, topped with a bright pink glaze. Lemons are more reliable year round, but they are really at their peak from July to December. If you can source them, I recommend Meyer lemons – available from November.

BLOOD ORANGE VERSION

Makes 1 x 900 g (2 lb) loaf
   or a 29 x 10 x 7 cm (12 x 4 x 3 in) loaf

300 g (10½ oz/1½ cups) caster
   (superfine) sugar
150 g (5¼ oz) butter
zest of 3 blood oranges
3 eggs
300 g (10½ oz/2½ cups) plain
   (all-purpose) flour
¼ teaspoon salt
2 teaspoons baking powder
¼ teaspoon ground cardamom

175 g (6 oz/⅔ cup) double (heavy) cream

for the syrup
100 g (3½ oz/scant ½ cup)
   blood orange juice
100 g (3½ oz/½ cup) caster
   (superfine) sugar

for the glaze
180 g (6¼ oz/¾ cup) icing
   (confectioner's) sugar
30 g (2 tablespoons) blood orange juice

LEMON VERSION

Makes 1 x 900 g (2 lb) loaf
   or a 29 x 10 x 7 cm (12 x 4 x 3 in) loaf

300 g (10½ oz/1½ cups) caster
   (superfine) sugar
150 g (5¼ oz) butter
zest of 3 lemons
3 eggs
300 g (10½ oz/2½ cups) plain
   (all-purpose) flour
¼ teaspoon salt
2 teaspoons baking powder

50 g (1¾ oz/¼ cup) poppy seeds
175 g (6 oz/⅔ cup) double (heavy) cream

for the syrup
100 g (3½ oz/scant ½ cup) lemon juice
100 g (3½ oz/½ cup) caster
   (superfine) sugar

for the glaze
180 g (6¼ oz/¾ cup) icing
   (confectioner's) sugar
30 g (2 tablespoons) lemon juice

Preheat the oven to 160°C (320°F/Gas 4). Grease and line a loaf tin.

Place the sugar, butter and your chosen zest into the bowl of a free-standing mixer and beat for about 5 minutes, until light and fluffy. Add the eggs, flour, salt, baking power and the cardamom or the poppy seeds, and mix until smooth, but avoid over mixing. Remove from the mixer and add in the cream, gently stirring by hand to combine. Spoon into the prepared loaf tin and bake for 45–50 minutes, or until a knife inserted into the middle comes out clean.

While the cake bakes, put the citrus juice and sugar for the syrup into a small pan over a medium heat. Simmer until the sugar has completely dissolved. Remove from the heat.

Once baked, allow the cake to cool in the tin for 10 minutes before turning out onto a cooling rack set on top of a baking (cookie) sheet. Using a skewer or cocktail stick, poke holes all over the top and sides of the cake. Brush the syrup all over the cake making sure you coat the full surface. Allow to cool.

To make the icing, slowly mix the icing sugar with the citrus juice to make a glaze that is thick but still pourable. Pour the glaze over the cooled cake, allowing it to drip down the sides.

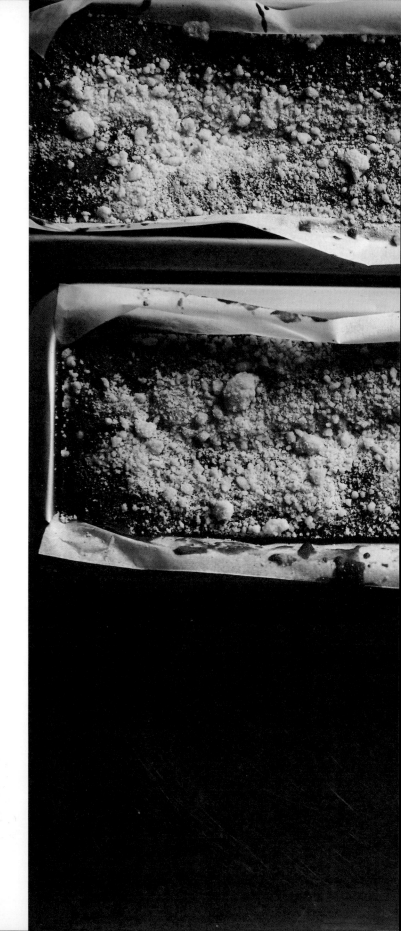

Apple crumble

APPLE CRUMBLE

We first developed this recipe as an attempt to wade our way through the bounteous apple crop we had in 2018. We were making four types of cake, jams, chutneys and tarts, and still found ourselves with tonnes of them at the end of each day. Thankfully, we eventually made our way to the bottom of the apple crate mountain; however, this cake hung around, and we continue to make it regularly. See recipe picture on pages 106–107.

Makes 1 x 900 g (2 lb) loaf
    or a 29 x 10 x 7 cm (12 x 4 x 3 in) loaf

400 g (14 oz) apples, skin on, grated
1 teaspoon ground cinnamon
100 g (3½ oz/⅔ cup) raisins or sultanas
    (golden raisins), soaked in boiling
    water for at least 30 minutes

225 g (8 oz) unsalted butter
225 g (8 oz/generous 1 cup)
    light brown sugar
3 eggs
225g (8 oz/1¾ cups) self-raising flour
½ teaspoon baking powder
½ quantity of Oat crumble (see page 227)

Preheat the oven to 160ºC (320ºF/Gas 4). Grease and line a loaf tin.

Toss the apple in the cinnamon until well coated. Set aside. Meanwhile, drain the raisins.

In the bowl of a free-standing mixer, beat the butter and sugar until light and fluffy. Add the eggs, flour and baking powder to the mixer and beat to combine. Fold through the raisins.

Spoon half of the mixture into your loaf tin and spread flat. Top with the apple (don't worry if it has browned slightly). Spoon the remaining mixture on top. Finish with the crumble. Bake for 30–40 minutes or until a skewer comes out of the middle clean. Allow to cool completely before removing from the tin.

BANANA, DATE AND CHOCOLATE

What we call the 'cyclist's cake', for both its robustness in a rucksack and also its ability to supply an unbelievable source of energy. Cooks and customers love it just as much, and let's face it, you need plenty of energy in our kitchen. See recipe picture on page 114.

Makes 1 x 900 g (2 lb) loaf
    or a 29 x 10 x 7 cm (12 x 4 x 3 in) loaf

250 g (8¾ oz/1⅓ cups) dried
    dates, chopped
250 g (8¾ oz/2¼ cups) light brown sugar
75 g (2½ oz) unsalted butter
250 g (8¾ oz/1 cup) water

2 eggs
2 bananas
275 g (9¾ oz/2¼ cups) self-raising flour
¼ teaspoon bicarbonate of soda
    (baking soda)
1 teaspoon vanilla bean paste
100 g (3½ oz) dark chocolate, chopped
¼ teaspoon salt

Preheat the oven to 160ºC (320ºF/Gas 4). Grease and line a loaf tin.

Place the dates, sugar, butter and water in a saucepan and heat gently until the sugar has fully dissolved and the butter has completely melted. Increase the heat and bring to the boil for just a second, then remove from heat immediately and let cool to room temperature. This normally takes a few hours, but you can place it in a sink full of ice-cold water to speed this process up a bit.

In a large bowl, mix the egg and banana together to form a chunky paste. Whisk in the cooled date mixture. Sieve in the flour, bicarbonate of soda, vanilla and whisk together. You don't want to overmix this batter, but do make sure the flour is well combined. Add the dark chocolate and the salt and fold through the mixture.

Pour the batter into the prepared tin and bake for 50 minutes–1 hour, or until a knife inserted in the middle comes out clean. Remove from oven and allow to cool in the tin for 15 minutes before turning out to cool completely on a wire rack. This is best served in thick wedges and slathered generously with butter.

PISTACHIO AND LIME

Humble, un-iced and simple in appearance, I love this recipe for its pure, unadulterated flavour. If you can source the expensive Iranian pistachios, use them to replace half of the regular nuts for the most brilliant colour loaf imaginable. You may, like me, have to re-mortgage your house in order to do so; however, it really is a great shade of green…

Makes 1 x 900 g (2 lb) loaf
    or a 29 x 10 x 7 cm (12 x 4 x 3 in) loaf

250 g (8¾ oz) unsalted butter, softened
225 g (8 oz/generous 1 cup) caster
    (superfine) sugar
zest of 1 lime
1 teaspoon vanilla bean paste

125 g (4½ oz/1¼ cups) pistachio nuts
4 eggs
100 g (3½ oz/1 cup) ground almonds
125 g (4½ oz/1 cup) plain
    (all-purpose) flour
1 teaspoon baking powder
¼ teaspoon salt

Preheat the oven to 160ºC (320ºF/Gas 4). Grease and line a loaf tin.

In the bowl of a free-standing mixer, cream together the butter, sugar, lime zest and vanilla until pale and fluffy. I use the whisk attachment for this recipe in order to get plenty of air into the mixture.

In the bowl of a food processor, blitz the pistachio nuts until they are fine and resemble the same consistency as the ground almonds. Remove from the processor and add to the creamed sugar mix along with the eggs, almonds, flour, baking powder and salt. Whisk until well combined and you have a pale and light batter. Spoon the batter into the prepared tin, then place in the oven and bake for 50–60 minutes, or until the sponge feels firm to the touch and a knife inserted into the middle of the loaf comes out clean.

Allow the loaf to cool a little in the tin, then turn out onto a wire rack to cool down fully. We like to serve this plain with only a little icing (confectioner's) sugar, or with fresh figs and natural yoghurt.

ICED GINGERBREAD

This is the first cake we baked at Aran, and an Angus original. A firm favourite and a very familiar bake if you have a Scottish granny. This recipe is for Ali Robb, who without fail will comment if I have been a bit stingy with the amount of buttercream. See recipe picture on page 114.

Makes 1 x 900 g (2 lb) loaf
  or a 29 x 10 x 7 cm (12 x 4 x 3 in) loaf

150 g (5¼ oz) unsalted butter
200 g (7 oz/1¼ cups) golden syrup
200 g (7 oz/1¼ cups) treacle
125 g (4½ oz/⅔ cup) light brown sugar
1½ teaspoons ground ginger
1 teaspoon mixed spice
½ teaspoon ground cinnamon
300 g (10½ oz/2½ cups) plain
  (all-purpose) flour

1 teaspoon bicarbonate of soda
  (baking soda)
2 eggs
250 g (8¾ oz/1 cup) whole (full-fat) milk

to finish
Swiss buttercream, to decorate
  (see page 226)
chopped stem ginger and edible flowers,
  to decorate (optional)

Preheat the oven to 140°C (280°F/Gas 3). Grease and line a loaf tin.

Weigh out the butter, syrup, treacle, sugar and spices into a large saucepan and melt over a medium heat until you have a smooth and well combined mixture. Set aside to cool. Once the syrup and butter has cooled, whisk in the eggs and milk. If you do this while the mix is too hot it will scramble the eggs, so it is worth being patient for this.

Weigh out the flour and bicarb in a large bowl and whisk in the wet mixture. When combining the wet and dry ingredients, do this for as short a time as possible, until just combined. If you mix the batter excessively, the end result can be a little tougher than you want, so always err on the side of caution. Pour the finished batter into the prepared loaf tin and bake in the preheated oven for about 45–50 minutes, sometimes longer. It is ready when the cake springs back after being lightly pressed or a knife inserted into the middle of the cake comes out clean. Set aside to cool.

To finish you can either top with Swiss buttercream, or simply leave plain. A lemon icing would work well also. We like to decorate with slivers of chopped stem ginger in the shop and a few yellow pansies, but it is totally up to creative interpretation. I would be quite happy to enjoy a slab of this with a cuppa and no additions whatsoever.

BOB

Bob is a local joiner and arguably our most regular customer.
He visits at least once a day without fail, often twice, and orders
a black coffee, with cold water and a small spoonful of sugar.
He can be referred to as Robert, Boblet and Bobbington.
None of which we think he likes that much...

If you could only eat one thing from the bakery what would it be?
*An almond croissant. Apart from the fact I like almonds, they are
perfect because they have a crisp exterior and soft, sweet middle.*

Much like you?
Ha! Yes, my middle is getting softer the more croissants I eat...

Who is your favourite bakery employee?
Hebe, because she is so off the wall!

From left to right: Banana date chocolate; Lemon and poppy seed;
Pistachio and lime; Iced gingerbread; Apple crumble

BUTTERNUT SQUASH
AND BIRNAM HONEY

We do our absolute best to source as many local ingredients as possible, and always encourage customers to come through the door with any of their own goods. One day, we received a wonky squash from a local gardener and a couple of jars of Birnam honey from a lovely man called Mark, and we knew we had to combine them. This is a mash-up of the only three recipes I could find that contained more butternut squash than sugar (something I think is important when cooking with vegetables) and the end result is quite unique. Not dissimilar to a tea cake, the crumb is very soft, and perfect with a cup of Lady Grey tea.

Makes 1 x 900 g (2 lb) loaf
    or a 29 x 10 x 7 cm (12 x 4 x 3 in) loaf

125 g (4½ oz) butternut squash, peeled
    and roughly chopped (peeled weight)
sunflower oil, for roasting
125 g (4½ oz) unsalted butter
100 g (3½ oz/½ cup) soft brown sugar
50 g (1¾ oz/¼ cup) runny honey

1 egg
175 g (6 oz/1⅓ cups) self-raising flour
25 g (1½ tablespoons) ground
    almonds (optional)
50 g (1¾ oz/¼ cup) olive oil
75 g (2¼ oz/½ cup) golden raisins
zest of 1 orange
½ teaspoon mixed spice
Demerara sugar, for scattering

Preheat the oven to 160ºC (320ºF/Gas 4). Grease and line a loaf tin.

Tip the squash into a roasting tin and drizzle with a little oil, but with no seasoning, which will feel bizarre if your roast a lot of veg. Cook for 20 minutes or until soft and tender – it doesn't need to be too well coloured. We tend to roast a big batch, remove the amount needed for this recipe once cooked, then season the rest and use in salads (for inspiration, see page 140). Let the squash cool down before blitzing to form a smooth purée.

In the bowl of a free-standing mixer, beat the butter, sugar and honey until smooth and pale. Add the egg, flour, almonds, if using, and oil. Beat again until fully combined. Add the cooled purée, raisins, zest and spice and mix together by hand. Pour into the prepared tin, sprinkle generously with Demerara sugar and bake for 40–50 minutes, or until cooked through and a knife inserted into the middle comes out clean.

SHORTBREAD

This is a Scottish cookbook. I was never going to limit myself to only one shortbread recipe. These two are from the best bakers I know – you can decide which one you prefer. The methods are much the same; however, the resulting texture and consistency is different. My granny's recipe is more akin to a traditional shortbread, the sort that a lot of people will associate with their granny's. Hers tends to be quite crisp and is normally cooked a little longer than Angus'. She also uses the back of a fork to scratch a ridged surface on the top, which forms perfect little divots for the sugar to fill and cling on to. Angus' has a far softer texture and more melt-in-the mouth consistency. To be honest, it was much too difficult a call to pick between the two, so I will let you make that decision yourself.

GRANNY JOAN'S

140 g (5 oz/scant ⅔ cup) caster (superfine) sugar, plus extra for dusting
280 g (10 oz) unsalted butter
425 g (15 oz/3½ cups) plain (all-purpose) flour

ANGUS'

170 g (6 oz/¾ cup) caster (superfine) sugar, plus extra for dusting
280 g (10 oz) unsalted butter
280 g (10 oz/2¼ cups) plain (all-purpose) flour
170 g (6 oz/1¼ cups) cornflour (cornstarch)

Preheat your oven to 140ºC (280ºF/Gas 3). Grease and line a deep, 23 cm (9 in) square baking tin.

For the shortbread base, beat the sugar and butter until pale and well combined – I find a hand-held electric mixer works best for this, but if your butter is soft, you can do this with a wooden spoon. Once the sugar and butter mix is pale in colour, add the flour(s). Beat it again but only for a moment, until the mixture resembles sandy breadcrumbs. Tip the mixture into the lined tin, pressing down very lightly so it becomes level. Bake for 30–40 minutes, or until pale golden in colour and cooked through. Sprinkle with caster sugar immediately, then allow to cool for 15 minutes. Slice into your chosen shape, be it bars or squares, then cool completely before removing from the tin.

APRICOT, GINGER AND BLACK SESAME FLAPJACK

Much to Angus' disgust, you will notice a particular fondness for ginger in this book. I adore the stuff, but Angus less so.

This recipe was based on ginger-poached apricots that I made for pudding one summer. I served them with a seeded oat crumble and wanted to find a way of making that flavour combination in the shop. Angus rolled his eyes when I suggested more ginger…

Makes 12

250 g (8¾ oz) unsalted butter
250 g (8¾ oz/scant 1 cup) golden syrup
250 g (8¾ oz/1¼ cups) caster
   (superfine) sugar
500 g (1 lb 1½ oz/5½ cups) rolled oats
200 g (7 oz/generous 1 cup)
   dried apricots, chopped

1 teaspoon ground ginger
50 g (1¾ oz/¼ cup) stem ginger,
   finely chopped
25 g (1½ tablespoons) black sesame seeds
50 g (3 tablespoons) sunflower seeds
25 g (2 tablespoons) pumpkin seeds

Preheat the oven to 140°C (280°F/Gas 3). Grease and line a deep 20 cm x 30 cm (8 x 12 in) baking tin.

Melt the butter together with the golden syrup and sugar over a low heat. Once well combined, remove from the heat.

Stir in the remaining ingredients and mix well to make sure everything is evenly coated and dispersed. Tip into the prepared tin and press down firmly using a spatula or the back of a spoon. Bake for 20–30 minutes, or until lightly golden and just set, but do bear in mind it will firm up as it cools.

Allow to cool completely before slicing. We find a serrated knife works best for this job. Keep in an airtight container for up to one week.

5. TWALHOURES

On the hoof

This is the Scots term for midday. The spelling 'houres' indicates the pronunciation 'oors'. The beginning of lunch and our customers shift to those on the run, in need of fuel and speed. The bakery is at its busiest as people become hungry, plan and sort picnics, and dash to work, and – dangerously – we begin to sell out of sausage rolls.

(From top to bottom) Spinach, feta and fennel;
Black pudding; Pork, apple and sage

SAUSAGE ROLLS

These were first made famous by Frank Maxwell, an entertainingly loud man who raved about them in the pub one night a few days after we opened. His high decibels were heard by most of the village and we spent our first-year trading desperately trying to make enough sausage rolls to stop them selling out within the first hour. It was both a blessing and a curse (specifically if you ask Scott, who has spent days and days making the pesky little things); however, despite all this, I reckon we owe him a dedication. Thanks for making all that noise, Frank.

PORK, APPLE AND SAGE

Makes 12

plain (all-purpose) flour, for dusting
1 kg (2 lb 3¼ oz) puff pastry
1 egg, beaten
splash of milk
white sesame seeds, to decorate
piccalilli, mustard or chutney, to serve
watercress, to serve

for the filling
500 g (1 lb 1½ oz) good-quality
   sausages, casing removed
500 g (1 lb 1½ oz) minced (ground)
   pork belly
100 g (3½ oz/⅔ cup) breadcrumbs
1 small bunch fresh sage, finely chopped
grating of nutmeg
1 teaspoon salt
freshly ground black pepper
1 large Granny Smith apple, skin on, grated
1 egg

Preheat the oven to 180ºC (350ºF/Gas 6).

Put the sausage meat into a large mixing bowl and add the minced pork belly and the breadcrumbs and sage. Add a good grating of nutmeg, then scrunch together well with your clean hands. Once combined, add the salt and pepper, then the apple. Lastly, crack in the egg and mix again to combine.

On a floured work surface, roll the pastry out into a big rectangle measuring 60 × 48 cm (24 × 19 in). It will be roughly 2.5 mm thick. Cut into 12 rectangles measuring 20 × 12 cm (8 × 5 in) each. Roll roughly 100 g (3½ oz) of the pork mixture into a sausage shape, approximately 12 cm (5 in) long. Repeat with the rest of the mixture and lay each along the top edge of each rectangle.

Continued overleaf

Mix the egg and milk and brush the pastry with the mixture, then roll the patry around the sausage meat, starting from the top until all the pastry has been wrapped around to encase the meat. Press down gently to seal.

Pour the sesame seeds into a shallow dish. Brush the top of the sausage rolls with more of the egg and milk, then dip into the sesame seeds, making sure you get a good coating. Place on a baking (cookie) sheet and bake for 20–25 minutes, or until puffed, golden and cooked through. Serve with piccalilli, mustard or chutney and some watercress.

HAGGIS

Makes 12

1 kg (2 lb 3¼ oz) puff pastry
1 egg, beaten
splash of milk
poppy seeds, to decorate
piccalilli, mustard or chutney, to serve
watercress, to serve

for the filling
250 g (8¾ oz) good-quality sausages,
    casing removed

250 g (8¾ oz) minced (ground) pork belly
500 g (1 lb 1½ oz) haggis (we use
    Macsween's), casing removed
100 g (3½ oz/⅔ cup) breadcrumbs
1 teaspoon mixed herbs, or finely
    chopped fresh parsley
grating of nutmeg
1 teaspoon salt
freshly ground black pepper
1 egg

Preheat the oven to 180ºC (350ºF/Gas 6).

Mix the sausage meat with the minced pork belly, haggis and the breadcrumbs in a large mixing bowl. Add the herbs and a good grating of nutmeg, then scrunch well with your clean hands until mixed together. Once combined, add the salt and a decent amount of black pepper, then crack in the egg and mix again.

On a floured work surface, roll the pastry out into a big rectangle measuring 60 × 48 cm (24 × 19 in). It will be roughly 2.5 mm thick. Cut into 12 rectangles measuring 20 × 12 cm (8 × 5 in) each. Roll roughly 100 g (3½ oz) of the haggis mixture into a sausage shape, approximately 12 cm (5 in) long. Repeat with the rest of the mixture and lay each along the top edge of each rectangle.

Mix the egg and milk and brush the pastry with the mixture, then roll the pastry around the sausage meat, starting from the top until all the pastry has been wrapped around to encase the meat. Press down gently to seal.

Pour the poppy seeds into a shallow dish. Brush the top of the sausage rolls with more of the egg wash, then dip into the poppy seeds, making sure you get a good coating. Place on a baking (cookie) sheet and bake for 20–25 minutes, or until puffed, golden and cooked through. Serve with piccalilli, mustard or chutney and some watercress.

SPINACH, FETA AND FENNEL

Makes 6

500 g (1 lb 1½ oz) puff pastry
1 egg, beaten
sesame and poppy seeds, for the topping
lemon wedges, to serve

for the filling
500 g (1 lb 1½ oz) spinach

1 teaspoon fennel seeds, plus extra
  for the topping
200 g (7 oz) feta, crumbled
2 spring onions (scallions), finely chopped
1 small bunch of parsley, finely chopped
75 g (2½ oz/½ cup) breadcrumbs
salt and freshly ground black pepper
grating of nutmeg

Preheat the oven to 180ºC (350ºF/Gas 6).

Wilt the spinach in a large frying pan (skillet) with a tiny splash of water. Once softened, remove and place in a tea towel. Squeeze to remove any excess water, then chop up finely. Set aside to cool.

Lightly grind the fennel seeds with a mortar and pestle. Place the cooled spinach, feta, spring onion, parsley, breadcrumbs, ground fennel seeds and salt and pepper to taste in a bowl and mix well to combine. Add a grating of nutmeg to taste and make sure you stir well.

On a floured work surface, roll the pastry out into a big rectangle measuring 60 × 24 cm (24 × 9½ in). It will be roughly 2.5 mm thick. Cut into 6 rectangles measuring 20 × 12 cm (8 × 5 in) each. Divide the spinach mixture into 6 even portions and roll into sausage shapes. Place down the middle of each pastry half and brush the edges with egg. Roll to enclose, ensuring the seam is underneath, and cut each roll in half.

Place on baking (cookie) sheets lined with non-stick baking paper, brush with egg and sprinkle with fennel, sesame and poppy seeds. Using a small, sharp knife, make slits in the tops of the rolls and bake for 25 minutes, or until golden. Serve with lemon wedges.

BLACK PUDDING

Makes 12

1 kg (1 lb 1½ oz) puff pastry
1 egg, beaten
splash of milk
black sesame seeds, to decorate
piccalilli, mustard or chutney, to serve
watercress, to serve

for the filling
250 g (8¾ oz) good-quality sausages,
    casing removed

250 g (8¾ oz) minced (ground) pork belly
500 g (1 lb 1½ oz) black pudding
    (we use Stornoway), casing removed
100 g (3½ oz/⅔ cup) breadcrumbs
1 teaspoon mixed herbs, or finely
    chopped fresh parsley
grating of nutmeg
1 teaspoon salt
freshly ground black pepper
1 egg

Preheat the oven to 180ºC (350ºF/Gas 6).

Mix the sausage meat with the minced pork belly, black pudding and the breadcrumbs in a large mixing bowl. Add the herbs and a good grating of nutmeg, then scrunch with your clean hands until well mixed. Once combined, add the salt and a decent amount of black pepper, then crack in the egg and mix again.

On a floured work surface, roll the pastry out into a big rectangle measuring 60 x 48 cm (24 x 19 in). It will be roughly 2.5 mm thick. Cut into 12 rectangles measuring 20 x 12 cm (8 x 5 in) each. Roll roughly 100 g (3½ oz) of the haggis mixture into a sausage shape, approximately 12 cm (5 in) long. Repeat with the rest of the mixture and lay each along the top edge of each rectangle.

Mix the egg and milk and brush the pastry with the mixture, then roll the pastry around the sausage meat, starting from the top until all the pastry has been wrapped around to encase the meat. Press down gently to seal.

Pour the black sesame seeds into a shallow dish. Brush the top of the sausage rolls with more of the egg wash, then dip into the sesame seeds making sure you get a good coating. Place on a baking (cookie) sheet and bake for 20–25 minutes, or until puffed, golden and cooked through. Serve with piccalilli, mustard or chutney and some watercress.

Black pudding sausage roll

MORNING ROLLS

These rolls have been remarkably popular. Contrary to classic Scottish fare they are not soft, white and floury, instead chewy, crisp and crunchy with seeds. We fire them well for flavour which is borderline blasphemy when it comes to the traditional roll or bap in these parts. Regardless, we love them and thankfully so do our customers.

Makes 8

300 g (10½ oz/1¼ cups) warm water
250 g (8¾ oz/2 cups) strong white bread flour, plus extra for dusting
250 g (8¾ oz/2 cups) granary flour
10 g (2 teaspoons) dried instant action yeast
10 g (2 teaspoons) salt
sunflower oil, for greasing
small handful of pumpkin, linseed, sunflower and poppy seeds
semolina, for dusting

Place all the ingredients except the oil, seeds and semolina in a free-standing mixer. Mix on a medium speed for 10 minutes until the dough is smooth and elastic. If doing this by hand, knead for 15 minutes. The more you work this dough the better, as it will help them hold their shape when proving and stop them from flattening in the oven. Set the dough aside in a lightly oiled bowl to prove for 30–45 minutes or until nearly doubled in size.

After the first prove, knock back on a lightly floured surface and divide the dough into 100 g (3½ oz) balls. Roll underneath the curve of your hand to form a tight ball.

In a bowl, mix together the seeds – you can use whatever combination you prefer. Grease and line a baking (cookie) sheet with greaseproof paper and dust with semolina. Brush the tops of the rolls with a little more water, then holding them by the base dip the wet tops into the seed mix. Place on the prepare baking sheet, making sure you space them out a little. The semolina helps if you need to move the rolls if they are joining together or proving too close to each other.

Prove for a further 30–45 minutes or until doubled in size and slow to spring back when gently touched. During this time, preheat the oven to its hottest possible setting, roughly 230ºC (450ºF/Gas 9).

Once proved, bake for 20 minutes until dark golden brown and hollow sounding when tapped underneath. Eat on the day of baking with a filling of your choice (see options on the next page).

These are our little 'pre-lunch' sandwiches. They are smaller than our sourdough-based sandwiches, but they do a grand trick when filling a little hungry gap. Or, if you are like my other half, James, then three in quick succession will sort you out for dinner.

PASTRAMI, COMTÉ AND GHERKIN

Coarsely grate some Comté, slice a gherkin and stack up tall in the roll with some pastrami.

PEA AND MINT HUMMUS WITH FETA AND PUMPKIN SEEDS

Blitz equal parts chickpeas (garbanzo beans) and peas with a little extra virgin olive oil, garlic and a small spoonful of tahini. Once smooth, add some lemon juice and some fresh mint and blitz again. Season or add more lemon or mint to taste. Spread over half of the roll then crumble over a little feta and some pumpkin seeds. Finish with some herbs and leaves.

MATURE CHEDDAR, PICCALLILI AND CORNICHON

Finely slice some good quality mature Cheddar and halve a few cornichons lengthways. Spread a roll with a little mayo and fill with Cheddar and the cornichons. Slather on a generous portion of piccalilli and finish with some rocket (arugula) or watercress. This is very good with smoked ham, too.

FRITTATAS

A joy to make and even tastier to eat. I love their simplicity and also speed. Although it seems like there are many elements on the go with these recipes you can have a delicious meal that will do breakfast, lunch and tea in under an hour. The excitement comes when you have to turn them out... Recipes are pictured overleaf.

LEEK, NEW POTATO, WILD GARLIC AND CHEDDAR

Serves 6 generously

400 g (14 oz) new potatoes, quartered
extra virgin olive oil, for frying
400 g (14 oz) leeks, finely sliced
100 g (3½ oz) wild garlic, spinach or nettles,
    finely chopped
8 eggs

double (heavy) cream,
    see method for quantity
100 g (3½ oz) Parmesan, coarsely grated
100 g (3½ oz) Cheddar, coarsely grated
salt and freshly ground black pepper
grating of nutmeg
1 small bunch of parsley, chopped
salad leaves, to serve

Preheat the oven to 170ºC (340ºF/Gas 5).

Bring a large pan of salted water to the boil and drop in your potatoes; they should only take 10–15 minutes to cook.

Heat a large ovenproof non-stick frying pan (skillet) – ours is 28 cm (11 in), but you can make an extra-deep frittata in a smaller pan – with a little olive oil. Cook the leeks until they are softened. Add the wild garlic and cook until the leaves wilt. Remove from the heat for a moment.

Crack the eggs into a measuring jug. Top up with double cream to the 800 ml (27 fl oz) mark. Add the grated cheeses and whisk. Season well and add a good grating of nutmeg. Fold through the parsley.

Drain the cooked potatoes and add to the pan along with a little extra oil. Return to the heat and pour in the cheese and egg mixture. Stir to make sure everything is coated. Fry over a medium heat for 5 minutes until the eggs start to settle and cook. Reduce the heat to low and cook for a few more minutes, then place in the oven for 10 minutes, or until cooked through. Allow to cool for 15 minutes, then cover with a plate and flip the pan carefully. Remove the pan and cover with a second plate. Flip over again and remove the top plate. Allow to cool completely before slicing. Best served with a tangle of salad.

CHANTERELLE, SHALLOT AND GRUYÈRE

Serves 6 generously

300 g (10½ oz) new potatoes, quartered
extra virgin olive oil, for frying
300 g (10½ oz) shallots, finely sliced
1 garlic clove, finely sliced
200 g (7 oz) chanterelle mushrooms,
    brushed, cleaned and trimmed
knob of butter

8 eggs
double (heavy) cream,
    see method for quantity
100 g (3½ oz) Gruyère, grated
100 g (3½ oz) Cheddar, grated
salt and freshly ground black pepper
grating of nutmeg
1 small bunch of thyme, leaves picked
salad leaves, to serve

Preheat the oven to 170ºC (340ºF/Gas 5).

Bring a large pan of salted water to the boil and drop in your potatoes; they should only take 10–15 minutes to cook.

Heat a large ovenproof non-stick frying pan (skillet) – ours is 28 cm (11 in), but you can make an extra-deep frittata in a smaller pan – with a little olive oil. Cook the shallots until softened, around 5 minutes. Add the garlic, cooking for a few minutes more. Tip out of the pan and into a bowl, then set aside.

Wipe out the pan, then place on a high heat and cook the chanterelles for a few moments. They will be squeaky to start with but will soften quite quickly. Once softened, around 3–5 minutes, add the butter and stir well. Return the onions and garlic to the pan, then turn off the heat.

Crack the eggs into a measuring jug. Top up with double cream to the 800 ml (27 fl oz) mark. Add the grated cheeses and whisk. Season well and add a good grating of nutmeg. Fold through the thyme.

Drain the cooked potatoes and add to the pan along with a little extra oil. Return to the heat and pour in the cheese and egg mixture. Stir to make sure everything is coated. Fry over a medium heat for 5 minutes until the eggs start to settle and cook. Reduce the heat to low and cook for a few more minutes, then place in the oven for 10 minutes, or until cooked through. Allow to cool for 15 minutes, then cover with a plate and flip the pan carefully. Remove the pan and cover with a second plate. Flip over again and remove the top plate. Allow to cool completely before slicing. Best served with a tangle of salad.

Leek, new potato, wild garlic and Cheddar frittata (left) and
An ode to Guardswell frittata (right)

AN ODE TO GUARDSWELL

Guardswell Farm is a beautifully renovated steading designed by Building Workshop, and run by the magical Anna Lamotte. Team Aran spent a glorious day there as a small treat a few weeks before our production kitchen was up and running. Here is my interpretation of the wonderfully fresh herb frittata that Anna made for us for lunch. It will always remind me of a wonderful day spent with the team that started it all.

I would also like to thank the very lovely Innes, who lives up the hill from the bakery and who provides us with a bounty of perfect herbs and leaves on a daily basis, many of which we use for this frittata. He appears early doors, smile on his face and endlessly generous with his offers. I worry that we would be a very beige establishment without his greenery.

Serves 6

extra virgin olive oil, for frying
1 shallot, finely chopped
1 leek, finely chopped
8 eggs
1½ teaspoons salt
freshly ground black pepper
1 teaspoon baking powder

grating of nutmeg
250 g (8¾ oz) herbs, very finely chopped
    (ideally blitzed in a food processor) –
    coriander (cilantro), dill, parsley
    and mint all work well
minted yoghurt, to serve
salad leaves dressed with lemon
    juice, to serve

Preheat the oven to 170°C (340°F/Gas 5).

Heat a little olive oil in a large frying pan (skillet). Add the veg to the pan and cook until softened and beginning to caramelise, around 8–10 minutes. Transfer to a plate and let cool. Wipe out the pan with paper towels.

Whisk the eggs, salt, a little pepper, baking powder and a grating of nutmeg in a large bowl. Using a rubber spatula, mix in the onion mixture. Add your fresh herbs to the bowl and combine. Your mixture should be thick and very green.

Add a little more oil to the same frying pan and place over a medium heat. Pour in the egg mixture and make sure it evenly coats the pan. Depending on how finely you have chopped the herbs, a spatula might help with this job. Turn the heat down to low and cook the frittata for roughly 5 minutes. Place in the preheated oven, watching carefully, until the top is just set, and starting to colour, roughly 5 minutes more. Let cool slightly, then gently loosen the sides. Either flip over to release from the pan or, if possible, slide out onto a platter. Allow to cool completely before serving with minted yoghurt and some lemon-spiked leaves.

INNES

Innes, our local herb chief and green-fingered hero, visits the bakery in the early hours of the morning when we have just started on the scones. He arrives laden with herbs and flowers, all of which are undeniably perfect having been grown in the slightly fickle Scottish climate. The quantity is impressive and we now refer to our shelving area as the herb garden due to its vibrant green nature. They are used bountifully in salads and to top our focaccia and frittatas, while his edible flowers sit pretty on top of our tartlets.

If you could only eat one thing from the bakery what would it be?
The classic sourdough. It reminds me of the very best southern French bakeries.

And if you could only grow one herb?
Fennel fronds – they are very versatile and touchy-feely in texture too!

Who is your favourite bakery employee?
Your mother, because she is my age! [Moments later Innes came back into the bakery to tell us it's also because she has a gorgeous smile, but we best not tell her that…]

6. LÒN

Lunch

Scottish Gaelic, masc. noun, meaning 1. food, provisions, repast, sustenance, victual, 2. lunch

Customers with time and empty stomachs begin to arrive. Feasts of door-stop sandwiches and mountains of salads become the most popular choices and people settle in their seats, happy to spend the next few minutes or hours stuffing themselves, and rightfully so. Many coffees are made. The bakers begin to wind down, cakes are cooling on all available surfaces and the following day's menu is planned. Sourdoughs prove determined and enthusiastically before their long sleep. It's been a busy day.

SALADS

We started the salad counter at the bakery quite early on. Much like the rest of the world, I was endlessly inspired by Ottolenghi's heaving great platters of glorious veg and grains. I love the concept of mixing and matching options and hate to be confined to only one choice. Whether or not this style would be a hit in little old Dunkeld was unknown to me; however, it quickly became our most popular savoury option and salads would sell out in the blink of an eye. We are wonderfully lucky to have a community-led initiative operating just up the road from the bakery called The Field. Run by volunteers, they grow a brilliant and bonkers variety of fruit and veg, all of which we incorporate into our salads. Every Saturday lunchtime, once their market stall has finished up for the day, a lovely basket of any excess bounty is brought to the bakery for us to use up the odds and ends. Last year, we were faced with beetroot (beets) by the bucket load, and before that there were courgettes (zucchini) covering every spare work surface. I love it like that. It forces creativity, and is a reassuring confirmation that nothing will go to waste.

Our salads change daily and are always accompanied by a big hunk of our fresh bread and plenty of butter, a reoccurring theme by this point in the day... I always choose the country loaf; however, customers can choose whichever loaf they fancy to sit alongside their little or large bowls stuffed full with colour.

A brilliant salad is all about variety and balance, so we use this handy and simple guide to help us formulate each day's options. They are always spontaneous and based on the produce we have to hand, and sometimes the volume of it. We view the salads as a meal on their own as opposed to a side dish; however, you could easily adapt this formula for side dishes – I would simply suggest cutting down on the grain element, as this does tend to make them more hearty and filling.

As you can see, this isn't a particularly specific guide and contains zero professional terminology, but this is how we cook and bake at Aran. In my opinion, this is how it should be. In the kitchen, you should always be instinctive and base your creations predominantly on taste and enjoyment. I don't think we would do it otherwise!

TO BEGIN
BULKINESS (1 part)
We use grains and pulses (legumes) as the main bulk for our salads. They provide a brilliant blank canvas for a variety of other flavours and contribute texture right from the start.
QUINOA, LENTILS, CHICKPEAS (GARBANZO BEANS), BULGAR WHEAT, MILLET, PEARL BARLEY, COUSCOUS, BUTTER (LIMA) BEANS, TOASTED BREAD, RICE

THE STARRING ROLE
TASTINESS (1 part)

This is the main element of the salad, and an ingredient you want to showcase. Think carefully about contrasting its texture with your BULKINESS and, for aesthetic reasons, also its colour. Often we use veg that has been cooked, roasted, fried or even finely sliced for this, to add an extra level of interest.

SLICED FENNEL, CHARRED TENDERSTEM (BROCCOLINI), ROASTED BUTTERNUT SQUASH, COOKED BABY CARROTS, FRIED HEIRLOOM TOMATOES, SPICED CAULIFLOWER, COURGETTE (ZUCCHINI) RIBBONS, GRILLED ASPARAGUS, CARAMELISED SHALLOTS, JULIENNED APPLE

THE SUPPORT ACT
LEAFINESS (½ part)

We adore everything green and leafy, be it a delicate herb, a peppery emerald shoot or a sturdy and robust leaf. They all have an important place in a salad.

MIZUNA, ROCKET (ARUGULA), SPINACH, KALE, LAMB'S LETTUCE (CORN SALAD), CAVOLO NERO (LACINATO KALE), WATERCRESS, CARROT TOPS, BABY GEM, RADICCHIO, BASIL, PARSLEY, DILL, TARRAGON, MINT

SOUND EFFECTS
CRUNCHINESS (½ part)

Texture is key when rounding off a salad, and something you should think about when building your layers.

TOASTED NUTS, SEEDS, RAW CARROT, TOASTED BREAD, RAW FENNEL BULB, CHICKPEAS (GARBANZO BEANS), PUFFED GRAINS, SPROUTED GRAINS

TO END
FRILLINESS (¼ part)

This is the pretty part. It should be as much about aesthetic as it is flavour. Think carefully about something that will contrast visually, and also consider it as a garnish to the dish – it must complement everything you have featured so far, but also be enough of a statement that it finishes the whole thing off.

MICROHERBS SUCH AS AMARANTH, BLACK SESAME SEEDS, POPPY SEEDS, CHILLI SLICES, CHOPPED HERBS, PEA SHOOTS, PARMESAN SHAVINGS, CRUMBLED FETA, TANGLE OF WATERCRESS, DUKKAH, TOASTED FLAKED (SLIVERED) ALMONDS, POMEGRANATE SEEDS, LEMON ZEST

This rough formula contains quite a few ingredients that can overlap in terms of their role and provide multiple textures and flavours. This isn't an issue and you should be able to see how flexible it is. There is more than enough scope to have two crunchy elements and more leaves than grains. We recommend to simply follow it as guide and not an exact science – your taste buds will do the rest.

ARAN HOUSE DRESSING

We make big jugs (pitchers) of this stuff each Wednesday before bottling it and using throughout the week on our toasts, in our salsa verde and, of course, to flavour our salads and grains. It will keep well, so I recommend scaling up and storing in the refrigerator for up to 1 month. As with all our recipes, we make this by metric weight. I find this far easier and a lot less messy.

Makes a 750 ml (51 fl oz/3 cup) bottle

500 g (1 lb 1½ oz/2 cups) olive oil
75 g (2½ oz/⅓ cup) freshly squeezed citrus juice
    (lemon or lime work best, but you can try grapefruit too)
125 g (4½ oz/½ cup) white wine or cider vinegar
1 garlic clove, minced
1 teaspoon good Dijon mustard
salt and freshly ground black pepper

Simply measure out all of the ingredients in one jug, whisk to your heart's content, then decant into a bottle or jar.

ROAST FENNEL, QUINOA, ORANGE AND SUNFLOWER SEEDS

This is an example of a salad with additions to the formula on pages 140–141. We have the bulk in the form of quinoa, the roasted fennel in the starring role, and orange as the support act. When it comes to tastiness, I think you can have as many elements as you fancy… mint and parsley provide some leafiness, sunflower seeds the crunch, and pretty slivers of red onion add frilliness, as well as a sharp kick.

I love to make this salad just as the seasons are beginning to change. It provides the comfort you need when either approaching or leaving winter, but has a freshness that makes it spring- and summer-like. Naturally, this is best enjoyed when the oranges are at their peak sweetness. The aniseed flavour of roasted fennel helps to further enhance the citrus.

Serves 4 as a main and 6 as a side

4 fennel bulbs, quartered
4 tablespoons extra virgin olive oil
4 tablespoons white wine vinegar
salt and freshly ground black pepper
250 g (8¾ oz/1¼ cups) quinoa
juice of 1 lemon
1 small red onion, finely sliced

Aran house dressing, to taste (see page 142)
4 oranges, peeled and sliced into discs, any escaping juice reserved (I like to use blood oranges when in season but regular are fine)
1 small bunch of fresh mint, leaves rolled up and sliced into ribbons
1 small bunch of parsley, finely chopped
75 g (2½ oz/½ cup) sunflower seeds

Preheat the oven to 180ºC (350ºF/Gas 6).

Arrange the fennel quarters in a roasting tin and drizzle with the olive oil and vinegar. Season lightly and toss together well. Roast in the oven for 15–20 minutes or until soft and tender.

While the fennel is roasting, place a pan of salted water over a high heat. Once boiling, cook the quinoa according to the packet instructions. Drain and set aside to cool.

Muddle the juice of the lemon and the red onion together in a small bowl to make a quick pickle. Leave for 10 minutes, then drain any excess liquid into the Aran house dressing along with any excess orange juice.

Once the fennel and quinoa have cooled, you are ready to assemble. Place all the ingredients in a large bowl and dress lightly. Toss together, then pile onto a large platter. Serve immediately with any excess dressing on the side.

KALE AND LENTIL SALAD
WITH BUTTERNUT

I love this salad for its dark colour and earthy flavours then spike of bright orange squash and pale, creamy crowdie. Kale gets all the attention by the clean-eaters, and I worry this sometimes puts people off it. Doused in a proper olive-oil dressing and accompanied by the meatiness of lentils and the crunch of almonds, it's the perfect meal.

Serves 4 as a main or 6 as a side

250 g (8¾ oz) butternut squash, peeled
    and sliced into 1 cm (½ in) half moons
2 small red chillies, finely sliced
2 garlic cloves, minced
extra virgin olive oil
salt and freshly ground black pepper
250 g (8¾ oz/1¼ cups) puy lentils

125 g (4½ oz) kale, stems removed
    and chopped roughly
75 g (2½ oz/½ cup) whole almonds,
    toasted and roughly chopped
1 small bunch of parsley, finely chopped
Aran house dressing, to taste (see page 142)
125 g (4½ oz) crowdie (Scottish curd
    cheese), feta or ricotta
fresh greens of choice, to serve

Preheat the oven to 180ºC (350ºF/Gas 6).

Place your butternut squash in a large bowl and toss through one of the chillis. Add the minced garlic and a generous slug of olive oil. Again, toss to combine. Tip onto a large baking (cookie) sheet, spreading everything out in order to allow it to cook evenly. Season lightly. Roast in the preheated oven for 20–25 minutes, or until soft and cooked through when a knife is pierced through the middle. Set aside to cool.

While your squash is cooking, start on the lentils. More often than not, I would recommend following the packet instructions for cooking; however, for lentils you can work on the basis of 3 times water to lentils. I do this by weight normally. Puy lentils will cook in roughly 20 minutes. A few minutes before the lentils are ready, add the kale to the pan and stir. Drain the lentils and the kale thoroughly, then set aside to cool.

Place the second finely sliced chilli in a large bowl. Use less if you don't want too much heat. Add the cooled squash, lentils and kale, making sure you scrape out any excess garlicky oil from the baking sheet. Add the almonds and parsley to the bowl and mix. Dress well using the Aran house dressing. Finely crumble in the crowdie and mix gently. Tip onto a serving platter and top with some greens of your choosing. Serve immediately.

TRISH

Trish is my lovely auntie and master of mischief. Endlessly helpful and always generous with her time, she sorts us out when we are short-staffed, regularly driving up from Edinburgh to save our sorry souls. Maker of a very mean bloody Mary and owner of many a great party outfit (the sequin bra remains a favourite), she is the member of staff that all others want to celebrate with.

Who is your favourite bakery employee?
Willow, because she is daft.

What is your favourite bakery good?
The salads because they are so varied.

What is your favourite bakery job?
Putting out the benches in the morning then sitting down on them for a roll-up!

. . . Least favourite job?
Washing up, natch.

Dunkeld salmon sandwich

*Tenderstem, harissa feta and avocado
with mizuna and toasted almonds sandwich*

SANDWICHES

We used to laugh when it came to sandwich time. Back in the early days, when we baked and prepared everything in our tiny little shop, Angus would more often than not be tasked with the sandwich prep. It was a job I don't think he enjoyed very much, as they would be all be sold before he even finished assembling them. He couldn't make them fast enough. To top the stressful sandwich situation off, I often forgot to add the fillings to our orders list. I would be so focused on the variety of flours, sugars, butters, oils and nuts I had to get, sandwich fillings would be the last thing on my mind. This meant that once the shop was stocked, cakes finished and the following day's sourdoughs were mixed (back then we did them by hand, a process I still miss), we would be faced with the prospect of what the heck to put in the sandwiches that day.

I would argue this made our sandwiches all the more creative. When we first put aubergine (eggplant) in a sandwich, my mum was particularly sceptical. But, alas, we had nothing else in our refrigerators, so we went for it. With some whipped lemon ricotta, it was a hit. The same could be said about our broccoli number. We were forced to be inventive, and I think it paid off.

Nowadays, they change weekly, are based on the seasons, wrapped in greaseproof ribbons and piled high on the counter. No plastic boxes or cling film (plastic wrap) in sight. They are normally sold out before 1 p.m. And, even better, I no longer have the responsibility of ordering fillings! Recipes pictured on pages 148–149 and 152–153.

TENDERSTEM, HARISSA FETA AND AVOCADO WITH MIZUNA AND TOASTED ALMONDS

Roast or steam your tenderstem broccoli (broccolini). Mix 1 teaspoon harissa for every 100 g (3½ oz) feta. The harissa feta can be made ahead of time and stores well in the refrigerator for up to 1 week. Pile the tenderstem onto the bread, top with a crumbling of feta, avocado slices, a handful of mizuna and some toasted almonds.

CUMIN-ROASTED AUBERGINE WITH LEMON, WHIPPED RICOTTA, SALSA VERDE AND ROCKET

Heat a non-stick frying pan (skillet) until hot, then place slices of aubergine (eggplant) in the pan. Do not add any oil. Once coloured slightly, place in a roasting tin and sprinkle with salt, pepper, cumin seeds and a little oil. Roast at 180°C (350°F/Gas 6) for 10–15 minutes until cooked through. Spread the bread with ricotta, add the aubergine slices, a drizzle of salsa verde and a handful of rocket (arugula).

SERRANO HAM, CELERIAC REMOULADE
AND WHOLEGRAIN MUSTARD WITH LEAVES

Coarsely grate some celeriac (celery root) and mix though mayonnaise, mustard (Dijon or wholegrain will work) and some lemon juice. Season to taste. Sandwich with a little more mustard, some salad leaves and plenty of good Serrano.

BACON, SOFT-BOILED EGG AND ROASTED
HEIRLOOM TOMATOES WITH WATERCRESS

Slice your tomatoes and place on a baking (cookie) sheet. Drizzle with oil, thyme leaves, salt and pepper and some bashed garlic cloves. Roast for 20 minutes at 180ºC (350ºF/Gas 6), or until soft. Soft-boil your eggs for 6 minutes. Place in cool water to stop the cooking process. Assemble the sandwich with some crispy smoked bacon, oozy eggs, a handful of watercress and the tomatoes.

DUNKELD SALMON

Begin by building your sandwich with a spoonful of crème fraîche on one piece of bread and a little mayo on the other. Top the crème fraîche with ribbons of cucumber, Fennel and orange pickle (see page 187) and some flakes of hot smoked salmon. I would always recommend Dunkeld Smoke House, if you can source it. Finish with fennel fronds and a crack of black pepper.

PEA AND NETTLE QUICHE

Nettles are steeped in culinary history. Apparently, 'nettle pudding' is the oldest recorded pudding in the books, but unlikely to make a reappearance, if you ask me.

I am all for nettles in savoury cooking, however, and even more so during this foraging renaissance. Here it's used in a spring quiche, and cooked much like you would spinach. It is important to make sure your nettles haven't been sprayed, and of course always wear heavy-duty gloves when handling.

Serves 10-12

plain (all-purpose) flour, for dusting
½ quantity of Savoury pastry (see page 228)
extra virgin olive oil, for frying
    and drizzling
2 shallots, finely sliced
1 big bunch of nettles, roughly 30 leaves
8 eggs

400 g (14 oz/1½ cups) double (heavy) cream
salt and freshly ground black pepper
1 bunch thyme, leaves picked
400 g (14 oz) peas
100 g (3½ oz) Parmesan, grated
1 bunch of parsley, finely chopped
    (chives or mint will work well too)
200 g (7 oz) ricotta
dressed leaves, to serve

Preheat the oven to 150°C (300°F/Gas 3).

On a lightly floured surface, roll out your pastry into a large round to fit a 30 cm (12 in) loose-bottomed tart tin, or a deep 27 cm (10 in) tin, with the pastry roughly 3 mm (⅛ in) thick. Transfer to your chosen tin and press the pastry into the edges and trim off any excess. Chill in the refrigerator while you prepare the filling.

In a frying pan (skillet) over a medium heat with a little olive oil, cook the shallots until caramelised, 8–10 minutes. Set aside to cool.

Blanch the nettles in boiling water for a minute before draining well. Roughly chop. Make sure you wear gloves when handling the nettles before they have been blanched.

In a large bowl, whisk together the eggs and cream with some seasoning and the thyme. Add the peas, nettles and shallots. Fold through the Parmesan along with the chopped herbs.

Pour into the chilled tart case and top with dollops of the ricotta, nestling them into the filling slightly. Drizzle with olive oil and top with a little black pepper. Bake for 40–50 minutes, or until golden brown on top and the base is completely cooked through. Allow to cool before serving with some leaves and dressing.

7. BLETHER

To share

Scottish, verb, meaning 1. talk in a long-winded way without making very much sense

Lunch slows down and cakes are now centre-stage. Old friends meet up for a blether, customers dash in for the last of the bread. Once more, the pace slows. Front of house staff also begin 'talking without making very much sense'. Back of house finish their day, placing orders for sacks of dry goods and flour and cleaning down.

PEAR, COFFEE AND HAZELNUT

Some of team Aran once ate this cake at the top of Clachnaben while enjoying a well-earned holiday in Aberdeenshire. I suspect it might have been the only reason we got back down again... that or the mugs of wine we gulped alongside it.

This is a nice wee twist on the classic. Don't get me wrong, I love a big traditional coffee cake stacked tall with buttercream and a million walnuts falling off it, but sometimes I like to get my sweetness from fruit on top rather than icing (frosting).

Serves 8-10

250 g (8¾ oz) unsalted butter
200 g (7 oz/1 cup) light brown sugar
50 g (1¾ oz/¼ cup) caster (superfine) sugar
200 g (7 oz/1½ cups) wholemeal (wholewheat) flour
50 g (1¾ oz/scant ½ cup) plain (all-purpose) flour
1½ teaspoons baking powder

4 eggs
125 g (4 oz/⅔ cup) hazelnuts
3 teaspoons instant coffee, mixed with 3 tablespoons boiling water, cooled
4 pears, unpeeled, cored and finely sliced, covered with apple juice to prevent browning
Demerara sugar, for scattering
crème fraîche or yoghurt, to serve (optional)

Preheat the oven to 160°C (320°F/Gas 4). Grease and line a 23 cm (9 in) cake tin.

Cream the butter and sugars together until light and fluffy. Add the flours, baking powder, eggs and 100 g (3½ oz) of the hazelnuts and set aside without mixing.

When ready to bake, add the cooled coffee to the cake mix and fold it all together until smooth. By mixing it later on (or as close to baking as possible) the baking powder won't activate too soon, and you will have a lighter texture when baked.

Pour into the lined tin. Working quickly, layer the pear on top of the cake mix and sprinkle with the remaining nuts and sugar. Put into the oven immediately. Bake for 40–50 minutes or until a skewer comes out of the middle clean. The majority of the pears will sink slightly into the cake, but don't worry as this will provide moisture.

Serve with some yoghurt or crème fraîche while still warm for a great pudding, or enjoy once cool with a cup of tea or coffee.

WHISKY ECCLES

A deeply untraditional rendition of the classic. However, as I am not from Eccles, perhaps I can be granted a small amount of creative licence? Moreover, when has whisky ever been a bad idea?

This recipe is dedicated to my dad, who refuses all sweet products, bar this one.

Makes 10-12

225 g (8 oz/1½ cups) raisins
zest of 1 orange
100 g (3½ oz/scant ½ cup) whisky,
    plus extra to serve (optional)
50 g (1¾ oz) unsalted butter

125 g (4½ oz/⅔ cups) light brown sugar
1 teaspoon ground allspice
1 teaspoon ground nutmeg
500 g (1 lb 1½ oz) puff pastry
caster (superfine) sugar, for dusting
2 egg whites, lightly beaten
cheese of your choice, to serve

Ideally the night before baking, mix together the raisins, orange zest and whisky. Set aside to soak. Alternatively, you can heat the whisky and pour over the fruit and leave for 1 hour until cool, but the flavour won't be as punchy.

On the day of baking, preheat the oven to 160°C (320°F/Gas 4).

To make the filling, melt the butter in a small saucepan over a low heat, before mixing in the sugar, allspice and nutmeg until well combined. Remove from the heat and stir in the soaked fruit and any excess juices. Set aside to cool.

Roll out the puff pastry until 4–5 mm (¼ in) thick and cut out as many 12 cm (5 in) circles as you can fit. Sadly, the nature of puff pastry means you can't normally re-roll it successfully, but we sometimes do some cobbled together Eccles cakes at the end – cook's perk! Spoon a dollop of cooled filling into the middle, and gather up the sides to cover the filling. Press together and seal with your fingers, then turn it over so it is seam-side down.

Fill a shallow dish big enough to fit in an Eccles cake with caster sugar. Brush the top of each cake with the egg white, then dip into the sugar. Slash the top of each cake 3 times. Apparently this is traditional, but by all means go for a single cut, a cross or anything else that takes your fancy. Bake for 15–20 minutes in the oven; keep an eye on them so that they don't burn.

Serve hot or cold with a big slab of cheese and, if you are in our house, a wee dram.

THE DEVIL'S DOUBLE

The darkest and richest cakes possible, both of these recipes serve their own purpose. I would recommend the Devil's food for birthday and celebration cakes alike, and the Chocolate rye cake (see page 163) for an after-dinner treat or as a grown-up pudding. Having said that, however, both are as brilliant as each other when enjoyed with an espresso (or something stronger) and a bit of peace and quiet.

DEVIL'S FOOD

Serves 8

50 g (1¾ oz/½ cup) cocoa powder
125 g (4½ oz/⅔ cup) caster
   (superfine) sugar
125 g (4½ oz/⅔ cup) light brown sugar
250 g (8¾ oz/1 cup) boiling water
125 g (4½ oz) unsalted butter, cubed
1 teaspoon vanilla bean paste

2 tablespoons brandy or coffee (optional)
2 eggs
250 g (8¾ oz/2 cups) self-raising flour
1 quantity of Chocolate ganache
   (see page 227)
rosemary sprigs, to decorate (optional)
icing (confectioner's) sugar,
   to decorate (optional)

Preheat the oven to 160ºC (320ºF/Gas 4). Grease and line a 20 cm (8 in) cake tin, ideally loose bottomed.

Weigh the cocoa, sugars, water and butter into a large bowl. Whisk well to combine, making sure everything is well incorporated. The smaller the butter is cubed, the faster it will melt into the mix. You can also use a hand-held electric mixer for this job. Add the vanilla and brandy or coffee, if using, into the bowl, then crack in the eggs. Finally, add the flour and mix well, making sure there are no lumps or little pockets of flour through the mixture. This drives my mum crazy!

Pour the mix into your prepared tin and bake in the oven for about 30–40 minutes, or until a knife inserted into the middle of the cake comes out clean. Allow to cool completely.

Once cooled, you can decorate with a thick layer of ganache spread on top. We like to spiral the icing then decorate with rosemary sprigs and icing sugar, but it would be equally as good slathered on top in any way you fancy.

CHOCOLATE RYE CAKE

Serves 8

100 g (3½ oz) dark chocolate,
    70% cocoa solids
100 g (3½ oz) unsalted butter
4 eggs
75 g (2½ oz/⅓ cup) caster (superfine) sugar

50 g (1¾ oz/¼ cup) light brown sugar
50 g (1¾ oz/¼ cup) rye flour
25 g (1½ tablespoons) cocoa powder,
    plus extra for dusting
6 tablespoons amaretto or Kahlúa
crème fraîche, to serve

Preheat the oven to 160ºC (320ºF/Gas 4). Grease and line a 20 cm (8 in) loose-bottomed cake tin.

Melt the chocolate and butter in a heatproof bowl over a half-filled pan of boiling water, making sure the bowl doesn't touch the water. Alternatively, you can do this directly over a very low heat, just be sure to stir it all the time to prevent the chocolate from burning. Set aside to cool.

In the bowl of a free-standing mixer, whisk the eggs and sugars until thick and pale. Mix the rye and cocoa together in a small bowl. With the mixer on a low speed, carefully add the cocoa mixture to the eggs, a spoonful at a time. Next, whisk your chosen booze into the cooled chocolate, then pour this mixture in a slow stream into the egg mixture.

Turn off the mixer, then stir gently by hand once fully combined to make sure no chocolate has sunk to the bottom. Pour into the prepared tin from a low height so as not to lose any aeration. Bake for 20–25 minutes, until the cake has nearly set but still has a wobble in the middle.

Allow to cool completely in the tin. Dust with a little cocoa, then serve with a big dollop of crème fraîche.

ARAN CARROT

For Kiri and 'Carrot Cake Jack' Pardoe, who are great friends of ours, and arguably only because of this cake. It has been used to celebrate everything from Jack's 30th birthday to their beautiful summer wedding down at the Cathedral.

Serves 8

250 g (8¾ oz/1 cup) vegetable
   or sunflower oil
250 g (8¾ oz) carrots, coarsely grated
250 g (8¾ oz/2¼ cups) light brown sugar
250 g (8¾ oz/2 cups) self-raising flour
4 eggs
100 g (3½ oz/⅔ cup) raisins or sultanas,
   (golden raisins) soaked in boiling water
   for at least 30 minutes, then drained

50 g (1¾ oz/scant ½ cup) pumpkin seeds
zest of 1 orange
1 teaspoon mixed spice
1 teaspoon ground cinnamon,
   plus extra to decorate
½ teaspoon ground nutmeg
Swiss buttercream, to decorate
   (see page 226)
orange zest, to decorate (optional)
chopped sunflower or pumpkin seeds,
   to decorate (optional)

Preheat the oven to 150°C (300°F/Gas 3). Grease and line a 20 cm (8 in) loose-bottomed cake tin.

Combine all of the ingredients, apart from the buttercream and decorations, in the bowl of a free-standing mixer and beat for a few minutes until smooth and well combined. This is a proper all-in-one method! Pour into your prepared cake tin and bake for 40 minutes or until a knife comes out of the middle clean. Allow to cool completely.

To decorate, cut in half and fill with a little Swiss buttercream. Level off the top, then add more buttercream on top. Alternatively, you can make a creamier icing (frosting) by stirring a little honey through mascarpone or cream cheese to taste. No matter what icing you are using, I would recommend adding a little orange zest and a small pinch of cinnamon to both. We like to dust the top with cinnamon and some chopped sunflower seeds or pumpkin seeds.

APRICOT AND ALMOND FRANGIPANI

This recipe was inspired by a tart I once saw made by The Little Duck Picklery, a restaurant in London. I never got to taste it, but was so thrilled by the concept of halved apricots (or any stone fruit) that I had to try it myself. I loved the idea of a big hunk of fruit in a tart – as opposed to fanned fruit, which often results in too high a filling-to-fruit ratio. It should always be half and half. Even more joyous are the little pools of sweet fruit juice from the pits where the stone once was. Simply magic.

Serves 10-12

½ quantity of Sweet pastry (see page 228)
1 quantity of Frangipane (see page 227)
150 g (5¼ oz) apricot jam
8-10 apricots, depending on size, halved and pitted
50 g (1¾ oz/½ cup) whole blanched almonds
Demerara sugar, for scattering
vanilla cream or amaretto cream, to serve

Preheat the oven to 160°C (320°F/Gas 4).

Roll out your sweet pastry to form a disc roughly 3 mm (⅛ in) thick and large enough to line a 30 cm (12 cm) loose-bottomed tart tin. Press the pastry into the fluted edge and trim off any excess. Set aside in the refrigerator to chill for 15 minutes. I use this time to make the frangipane.

Once the pastry is chilled, spoon the apricot jam into the base of the tart case and spread level. Next spoon on the frangipane filling. Place the apricots over the top of the frangipane, cut-side up. Squeeze in as many as you can. Sprinkle the whole almonds over the top and finish with some Demerara. Bake for 40–45 minutes, or until cooked through and the base is evenly golden. Allow to cool completely before slicing. Serve with softly whipped cream, which you can spike with either a little vanilla bean paste or some amaretto. You only need to add a little.

ANJA'S APPELTAART

Anja Baak set up Great Glen Charcuterie with her husband Jan Jacob around 10 years ago. All of their products are produced by hand and air-dried at their home in the Highlands, preserving as much of the unique and delicious flavour of wild venison as possible. I first met Anja not long after we established ourselves, as she would pop in and say hello on her various trips up and down the A9 road. It has always been a great joy to me how easily relationships form between independent businesses in Scotland, Anja's being the first example of this for us. Her green peppercorn salami features heavily in the bakery, sandwiched in between slices of sourdough with pickled red cabbage. All of us behind the counter are guilty of bolting down a great number of slices before it even gets to lunchtime.

On a recent trip to Amsterdam with my partner, I devoured a slice of nearly every single appeltaart available in order to recreate one for the bakery, which I so desperately wanted to do. I knew I had to ask Anja, who is originally from the Netherlands. She dutifully hand wrote her family recipe, and to my delight it was almost identical to those we enjoyed while away. After baking it only once, I very sadly lost her lovely hand-written recipe and spent weeks searching our production kitchen for it, to no avail. I have since learnt my lesson and, thanks to Anja's patience, I have the recipe once more – now it's in this book, it will never be lost again.

We are very fortunate to be surrounded by brilliant and like-minded producers throughout the country who are generous with both their time and wealth of knowledge. This story is a prime example of the diversity and generosity around us. See recipe picture overleaf.

Serves 8

250 g (8¾ oz/1¼ cups) caster
    (superfine) sugar
zest of ½ and juice of 1 lemon
250 g (8¾ oz) unsalted butter, plus extra
    for greasing
2 tablespoons cold water
500 g (1 lb 1½ oz/4 cups) self-raising flour
about 8 cooking apples, such as
    Bramleys, peeled and chopped into
    thumb-sized pieces
1½ teaspoons ground cinnamon
1 tablespoon custard powder or
    1 tablespoon cornflour (cornstarch)

small dash of vanilla bean paste
2 tablespoons apricot jam, plus extra
    to glaze
1 handful of raisins, or sultanas
    (golden raisins) if you can source
    them (optional)
1 egg, beaten
whipped cream, to serve

for the almond layer
4 tablespoons sugar
4 tablespoons ground almonds
1 egg

Begin with the pastry. In a small bowl, mix the sugar, grated lemon zest and butter until smooth, add 1 cold tablespoon of the water and mix again, then add the flour. When it is well mixed, add another cold tablespoon of water and use your hands to bring together. Cover and chill in the refrigerator for a few hours.

In a second bowl, mix the apples with the lemon juice, cinnamon, custard powder, and apricot jam. Set aside.

Next, mix the ingredients for the almond layer into a thick paste.

Preheat the oven to 160°C (320°F/Gas 4). Butter a shallow 20 cm (8 in) springform baking tin or pie dish.

Roll out half of your pastry dough into a large round to fit your tin, with the pastry roughly 3 mm (⅛ in) thick. Line the baking tin with this half of the pastry dough and set the other half aside. Gently spread the almond layer over the bottom. You can scatter this in if the paste is crumbly. Spoon the apple mixture on top as evenly as possible. Scatter over some raisins if using.

Using the remaining half of the pastry dough, roll out a round roughly 2 mm (⅛ in) thick. Cut the dough into even strips, roughly 2 cm (¾ in) thick, depending on how thick you want your lattice strips. Lay out 5 parallel strips on top of the filling, leaving equal space between them. Fold back every other strip so they are in half. Place another long strip where you have folded the others over so that the strip is at a 90-degree angle to the others. Unfold the folded strips over the individual strip. Now take the parallel strips that are running underneath the individual strip and fold them back over. Lay down a second perpendicular strip next to the first one, with some space between the strips. Unfold the folded parallel strips over the second strip. Continue this process until the lattice is complete. Trim the edges.

Brush with the beaten egg and bake for 1 hour, until golden.

When out of the oven, brush with some apricot jam, warmed through in a small saucepan. Leave to cool down in the tin.

Serve with whipped cream.

Anja's Appeltaart

Marshmallows

MARSHMALLOWS

Always fun to make and enjoyable to portion; nothing rivals the texture of homemade mallows. See recipe picture on page 173.

Makes 25

sunflower oil, for greasing
6 gelatine leaves
2 large egg whites
275 g (9¾ oz/1⅓ cups) caster
    (superfine) sugar

small pinch of salt
150 g (5¼ oz/⅔ cup) water
2 tablespoons golden syrup
2 tablespoons honey
cornflour (cornstarch), for dusting (optional)
icing (confectioner's) sugar,
    for dusting (optional)

Lightly grease and line a 20 cm (8 in) square tin and grease the greaseproof paper.

Place the gelatine leaves in a bowl of cold water and set aside to soak.

Place the egg whites in the bowl of a free-standing mixer fitted with the whisk attachment. Add 1 tablespoon of the caster sugar and a small pinch of salt, but don't whisk yet.

Combine the remaining caster sugar with the water, golden syrup and honey in a medium saucepan. Place over a high heat and bring to the boil, then simmer until the syrup reaches 115ºC (240ºF) on a sugar thermometer. Remove the pan from the heat. Working quickly, whisk the egg whites on high speed until stiff peaks form. Drain the softened gelatine and stir into the warm syrup mixture, whisking together until dissolved and fully combined. Slowly, with the mixer on a medium speed now, pour the syrup in a steady stream into the meringue. The mixture will grow in volume quite quickly. Once fully added, increase the speed to high and whisk for a further 5 minutes until thick and glossy. The bowl should no longer be hot to the touch. Pour into your prepared tin and gently level off the marshmallow with a palette knife.

Allow to cool completely at room temperature before covering with a thin coat of oil. Press another sheet of greaseproof paper on top then cover with cling film (plastic wrap) and leave to set until firm, about 4 hours, though ideally overnight.

To cut up the marshmallow we like to use scissors or a large knife and hot water to clean them in between. You will find it is a sticky business. If you are going to be eating the marshmallow within the next few days, you can make a small mixture of equal parts cornflour and icing sugar to coat them lightly and prevent sticking. However, we found if you do this, they tend to dry out after around 2–3 days. Instead, cut carefully and store in an airtight container, making sure the marshamllows are arranged so that they don't touch and stick to each other. If they do, simply use scissors to separate again. You can store them like this for up to 2 weeks.

GINGERBREAD

Mix 1 teaspoon ground ginger, 1 teaspoon allspice, 1 teaspoon cinnamon and ½ teaspoon mixed spice together. Add to the mallow mixture towards the end of whisking.

CHAMOMILE

Boil the water, before steeping 2 bags of chamomile tea in it until fairly strong. Remove the bags and proceed to make the syrup as usual. Once poured into the tin, sprinkle the top of the mallows with some dried chamomile flowers. Allow to set as usual but don't add any more oil to the top of the mallows.

VANILLA

Add 2 teaspoons vanilla bean paste to the mallow mixture towards the end of whisking.

CHOCOLATE OAT COOKIES

These cookies are delicious served warm for afternoon tea or late in the evening when you have a pang in your sweet-tooth. Simply store in the freezer, divided and flattened slightly as instructed in the recipe and bake from frozen.

Makes 24 cookies

275 g (9¾ oz/2¼ cups) plain
   (all-purpose) flour
2 teaspoons baking powder
1 teaspoon salt
400 g (14 oz/2¼ cups) rolled oats
350 g (12½ oz) unsalted butter, softened

175 g (6 oz/1¾ cups) light brown sugar
375 g (13¼ oz/1¾ cups) caster
   (superfine) sugar
2 eggs
1 teaspoon vanilla bean paste
200 g (7 oz) dark chocolate chips
200 g (7 oz) white chocolate chips
   (or more dark)

Preheat the oven to 160ºC (320ºF/Gas 4). Grease and line 2 large baking (cookie) sheets.

In a decent-sized bowl, mix together the flour, baking powder, salt and oats.

In the bowl of a free-standing mixer, beat together the butter and the sugars until creamed but not too light and fluffy. This should only take 1–2 minutes – remember you are making cookies, not a sponge, so don't worry too much about aeration. Add the eggs and the vanilla and beat again until just combined. Finally, add the dry ingredients you mixed earlier and the chocolate chips. Mix until combined. At this point, you can chill the dough in the refrigerator for an hour or so until you are ready to bake. Alternatively, you can make them straight away.

Use a set of scales to weigh out your cookies – this allows for consistency and also makes sure your cookies are all even from a cooking perspective – no one wants an overcooked number. We scale all of our cookies to 85 g (3 oz) but this does make 24 quite large ones, so go for 45 g (1½ oz) for 48 smaller cookies. Once weighed out, roll each lump of dough into a ball. Place on a baking sheet (we allow 6 large ones per sheet as they do spread out quite a bit) and press down firmly, but don't squash entirely. Once flatted they should be about 15 mm (½ in) thick. (If you don't want to bake straight away, you can freeze them at this point.) Bake for 10–12 minutes before checking and baking for no more than a further 5–7 minutes. Soft and gooey is the aim, as they will firm up as they cool. If you like a crisp cookie, bake them a little more by all means, but on your head be it. If they aren't chewy when we put them out on the counter, there is guaranteed uproar. Cool on the baking sheet for 10 minutes, then transfer to a wire rack and leave until completely cooled. Store in an airtight container for up to 1 week.

8. PANTRY

On the shelves

During our afternoon lull, once customers have been looked after, we begin to potter around the shop and set about restocking our pantry shelves. Jams and chutneys are made, spices, pickles, and biscuits too. We take time sterilising endless jars and writing out labels in our best handwriting possible. Jam making is an endless circle of thinking you have plenty, then finding the last jar of the stuff only days later.

MACADAMIA AND STAR ANISE BISCOTTI

An excellent gift around Christmas time, but really these are tasty any time of the year. Serve with Vin Santo, for a crowd.

Makes 24

2 eggs
1 egg yolk
200 g (7 oz/1 cup) caster (superfine) sugar
1 teaspoon vanilla bean paste
25 g (1½ tablespoons) sesame seeds, black and white

300 g (10½ oz/2½ cups) plain (all-purpose) flour, plus extra for dusting
1½ teaspoons baking powder
1 teaspoon ground star anise
150 g (5¼ oz/⅔ cup) sunflower oil
150 g (5¼ oz/1 cup) macadamia nuts
50 g (1¾ oz/⅓ cup) flaked (slivered) almonds

Preheat the oven to 160°C (320°F/Gas 4). Grease and line a large baking (cookie) sheet.

In the bowl of a free-standing mixer, weigh out all of the ingredients. Beat together until just combined – you should have a fairly wet dough. Working quickly on a lightly floured surface, shape the dough into 2 equal logs, roughly 7 cm (3 in) wide. Carefully place side by side on the baking sheet, making sure you allow plenty of room for them to spread. Bake for 20–25 minutes or until golden brown and nearly cooked through. They will be quite flat, but don't worry. Allow to cool at room temperature for roughly 30 minutes.

Once cooled, use a serrated knife to cut diagonal slices down the length of each log. Your slices should be no more than 2 cm (¾ in) thick, though ideally 1½ cm (½ in). Arrange cut-side down on a baking sheet and return to the oven to crisp up. This shouldn't take any more than 15 minutes, but be sure to watch them as they can burn quite easily.

Allow to cool completely before wrapping in cellophane bags or storing in an airtight jar. They will last for up to 1 month.

AMARETTI

We serve little versions of these with our coffees in the shop. You can make them larger and use in puddings or broken up and folded through a semifreddo, but as someone who doesn't take sugar in their coffee, I quite like the small amount of sweetness a wee biscuit adds as an accompaniment to an espresso.

Makes 48 small

200 g (7 oz/¼ cups) hazelnuts
2 egg whites
200 g (7 oz/1 cup) caster (superfine) sugar
50 g (1¾ oz/¼ cup) brandy
½ teaspoon vanilla bean paste
icing (confectioner's) sugar, for dusting

Preheat the oven to 180ºC (350ºF/Gas 6). Grease and line 2 baking (cookie) sheets.

Tip the hazelnuts onto a third baking sheet and toast for 2 minutes, or until golden brown and fragrant. Watch them carefully, as they do tend to catch quite easily. You can use blanched hazelnuts for this recipe; however, I tend to use skin-on as I quite like it when you can see flecks of colour from the skin through the amaretti. Both will work equally well, though. Set the hazelnuts aside to cool. Turn the oven down to 140ºC (280ºF/Gas 3).

In the bowl of a free-standing mixer, whisk up the egg whites until they form stiff peaks, much like a meringue. Begin gradually adding the sugar, mixer on a medium speed. I add this 1 tablespoon at a time. Make sure you wait for it to be fully incorporated before adding more. After 2 minutes, and once all the sugar has been added, the meringue should be thick and glossy looking. Place the cooled hazelnuts in the bowl of a food processor and blitz on a high speed until fine and resembling the consistency of ground almonds. Add to the meringue along with the brandy and vanilla. Fold the nuts through the mixture until it is well incorporated. Transfer to a piping (pastry) bag fitted with a plain nozzle. Pipe small rounds, roughly 2 cm (¾ in) across, on the prepared baking sheets. Use a sieve to dust icing sugar over the surface of the amaretti. Bake for 10–15 minutes until golden brown and slightly cracked. Allow to cool completely, then store in an airtight container for up to 4 weeks.

FENNEL AND ORANGE PICKLE

I like to make this pickle in smaller jars as it is far more practical for gifts, and shelf life. If you are making it for your own pantry or as we do for the shop, the below quantities will fill one or two large Kilner-(Mason-) style jars. Use in our hot smoked Dunkeld salmon sandwiches (see page 151). This is also delicious when tossed through a salad.

Makes 4 x 300 g (10½ oz) jars

4 small fennel bulbs, roughly
    500 g (1 lb 1½ oz), fronds reserved,
    finely sliced horizontally with
    a mandolin or food processor

for the brine
350 g (12½ oz/scant 1½ cups) white
    wine vinegar
350 g (12½ oz/scant 1½ cups) water

150 g (5¼ oz/⅔ cup) caster (superfine)
    sugar
2 teaspoons chilli flakes
2 teaspoons yellow mustard seeds
1 teaspoon salt
1 teaspoon black peppercorns
peel of 2 oranges, very thinly sliced
peel of 1 lime, very thinly sliced
small bunch of fennel fronds (reserved
    from the bulbs) or dill

Wash the jars and lids with hot soapy water then put in a roasting tin and place into an oven heated to 130ºC (280ºF/Gas 2) for about 15 minutes. Do the same with any utensils that will come into contact with the pickle and jars once boiled (for example we use a jam funnel and a small ladle to transfer the brine) to make sure these are sterilised properly also.

Place all the ingredients for the brine, except for the citrus peel and the fennel fronds, in a saucepan and bring to the boil. Once the sugar has completely dissolved, remove from the heat. Stir in the orange zest, lime zest and fennel fronds. Fill each jar with as many fennel slivers as you can squeeze in. Pour the hot brine on top, making sure you distribute the citrus and fronds evenly between the jars. Seal immediately and store in a cool dark cupboard. These are best kept for a few weeks before tucking in. Store in the refrigerator for up to 1 month once opened.

PROSECCO TRUFFLES

I spend the vast majority of my time in the kitchen trying to smuggle in booze and nuts to recipes. I failed with the nuts with these truffles but by all means roll them in some toasted hazelnuts if you like. Whether it is fashionable/sensible or not, prosecco is my go-to drink, so it seemed fitting to include it at least once.

Makes 24

650 g (1 lb 7 oz) dark chocolate
  (more than 54% solids)
100 g (3½ oz/scant ½ cup) double
  (heavy) cream

100 g (3½ oz) unsalted butter
100 g (3½ oz/scant ½ cup) prosecco
2 tablespoons brandy or amaretto
cocoa powder, for dusting
sea salt flakes

Weigh out 225 g (8 oz) of the chocolate in a bowl and set aside. Put the cream and butter into a small saucepan and place over a medium-high heat. As soon as they come to the boil, pour them over the chocolate. Leave for 2 minutes, then whisk together gently to melt and combine, then whisk in the prosecco. Set aside for 1 hour, or until the mixture is firm and spreadable. Unlike the Chocolate ganache (see page 227), we don't recommend speeding this process up in a chilled sink of water as it makes the mixture uneven in texture.

Once cooled, transfer the mix to a piping (pastry) bag fitted with a wide, plain nozzle and pipe long logs of the mixture onto a greased and lined baking (cookie) sheet. Place in the refrigerator for 30 minutes, or until completely set. Chop into small 2 cm (¾ in) truffles once chilled.

Tip some cocoa powder into a small shallow bowl. Melt the last 100 g (3½ oz) of chocolate in a small glass bowl over a pan of simmering water. Dip one truffle at a time into the chocolate to lightly coat, then drop the truffle into the cocoa powder and roll gently to seal the chocolate. Work fast to stop the chocolate setting too quickly; this is a messy business, so consider yourself warned. Place on a second baking sheet and chill for 30 minutes, until set.

Shake off any excess cocoa and then serve, or alternatively wrap in little cellophane bags or in a small gift box. They will keep, sealed and chilled, for up to 2 weeks.

PICKLED GREEN TOMATOES

These are apparently very popular in Italy, although I'd never heard of them until a few summers ago. This recipe was devised solely out of necessity when we found ourselves with a bounty of them at home. Deliciously tart served on toast with ricotta, hazelnuts and sweet cherry plum tomatoes.

Makes 6 × 300 g (10½ oz) jars

750 g (11 lb 10½ oz) green tomatoes, quartered

for the brine
500 g (1 lb 1½ oz/2 cups) white wine vinegar

500 g (1 lb 1½ oz/2 cups) water
350 g (12½ oz/1¾ cups) caster (superfine) sugar
1 tablespoon yellow mustard seeds
2 teaspoons chilli flakes
2 garlic cloves, cut in slivers
2 teaspoons whole black peppercorns
2 teaspoons salt

Wash the jars and lids with hot soapy water, then put in a roasting tin and place into an oven heated to 130ºC (280ºF/Gas 2) for about 15 minutes. Do the same with any utensils that will come into contact with the pickle and jars once boiled (for example we use a jam funnel and a small ladle to transfer the brine) to make sure these are sterilised properly also.

Place all the ingredients for the brine in a saucepan and bring to the boil. Once the sugar has completely dissolved, remove from the heat.

Fill each jar with as many tomatoes as you can squeeze in. Pour the hot brine on top. Seal immediately and store in a cool dark cupboard. These are best kept for a few weeks before tucking in. Store in the refrigerator for up to 1 month once opened.

CRAB APPLE AND ROWAN BERRY JELLY

The number of jars you require depends on how much juice you yield from the fruit. I normally get roughly 6–8 × 200 g (7 oz) jars from this recipe. Smaller jars are best for this because the jelly tends to set and keep better. Leave the cores of the crab apples intact as they contain lots of pectin, which will improve the set on your jelly.

6-8 × 200 g (7 oz) jars

500 g (1 lb 1½ oz) rowan berries, washed, stalks and twigs removed
1.5 kg (3 lb 5 oz) crab apples, quartered
750 g (1 lb 10½ oz/3 cups) water
1–2 kg (2 lb 3 oz–4 lb 6½ oz/5-10 cups) granulated sugar

Place all the fruit in a large heavy-bottomed saucepan along with the water. Bring to the boil and simmer, stirring regularly in order to help break down the fruit. You should have a pulp-like consistency.

Tip the mixture into a jelly bag (or a large sieve lined with a muslin cloth) suspended over a bowl and leave to drain. Try not to force any liquid through as this will affect the clarity of your jelly. This can take hours, so I often leave it overnight.

Once the liquid has stopped dripping through the cloth, measure the juice, then transfer it to a clean pan. For every litre of juice add 750 g (1 lb 10½ oz/3¾ cups) of the sugar. Place over a medium heat until the sugar has dissolved, then bring to the boil. Skim off any scum that rises to the surface. The setting point for this jelly is 106°C (225°F). Alternatively, use the wrinkle test. Spoon a little jelly onto a cold saucer, put this in the refrigerator for a couple of minutes, then push your finger through the jelly. If the surface wrinkles, your jelly is ready. If it remains liquid, boil for another 5–10 minutes, then repeat.

While the chutney is cooking, wash the jars and lids with hot soapy water, then put in a roasting tin and place into an oven heated to 130°F (280°F/Gas 2) for about 15 minutes. Do the same with any utensils that will come into contact with the pickle and jars once boiled (for example we use a jam funnel and a small ladle to transfer the jelly) to make sure these are sterilised properly also.

As soon as setting point is reached, remove the pan from the heat and pour the jelly into your warm, sterilised jars. Cover with a disc of greaseproof paper, then a lid. This jelly is best left for 1 month before you tuck in. Store in a cool dark place for up to 1 year and, once opened, keep in the refrigerator and use within 1 month.

COLIN'S APPLE CHUTNEY

Not one for the kitchen, my dad's contribution to the bakery has been mainly (and thankfully) dish washing. One Christmas, however, when we were overwhelmed, he astounded us all by making a huge batch of apple chutney to restock our increasingly empty shelves. People still ask about 'Colin's chutney' to this day.

Makes 8 jars

500 g (1 lb 1½ oz) shallots, finely chopped
olive oil, for frying
1.5 kg (3 lb 5 oz) apples, roughly chopped
750 g (1 lb 10½ oz/3 cups) malt vinegar
750 g (1 lb 10½ oz/3¾ cups) light
   brown sugar

250 g (1⅔ cups) raisins
1 teaspoon ground cloves
2 teaspoons ground coriander
2 teaspoons mixed spice
2 teaspoons salt

Place the shallots in a large saucepan with a slug of oil. Cook over a medium heat until softened but not caramelised, around 10 minutes. Add the remaining ingredients. Slowly bring to the boil until the sugar has dissolved. Allow to simmer over a low heat for roughly 1–2 hours, regularly stirring to prevent the bottom from sticking or burning.

While the chutney is cooking, wash the jars and lids with hot soapy water, then put in a roasting tin and place into an oven heated to 130°C (280°F/Gas 2) for about 15 minutes. Do the same with any utensils that will come into contact with the pickle and jars once boiled (for example, we use a jam funnel and a small ladle to transfer the chutney) to make sure these are sterilised properly also.

Once thick and you can draw a wooden spoon across the base of the pan so that it leaves a gap behind it that does not immediately fill with liquid, the chutney is ready. Transfer into your sterilised jars. Cover with small greaseproof paper discs then seal the lids tightly. Best stored in a cool, dark cupboard for 2–3 months before eating; however, we regularly dive in straight away. Once opened keep in the refrigerator for up to 1 month.

DAD (COLIN)

Colin, Dad, Daddy, 'Faither'. The only man I know to have turned up for a dish-washing shift in a smart shirt and woollen jumper. Despite sweating profusely he kept his jumper on throughout 'in case someone he knew came in'. In the bakery, we enjoy crops of his stripy beetroot and endless rocket bounty, and all love him dearly for his dry and direct sense of humour.

What is your favourite bakery good?
The sausage rolls, because they aren't cake.

Who is your favourite Aran employee?
I like them all and for some reason they all seem to like me. I don't know any of their names though…

. . . Favourite daughter?
Hebe, obviously.
[This is a constant sore point for me and has become a long standing joke ever since we were wee. Dad took the joke so far one time that he rewarded Hebe a tenner simply for 'not being Flora'. I, of course, rise to it every time.]

Least favourite thing about the bakery?
I always seem to be in the way due to its busy nature. Hence my brief visits!

SLOE VODKA

We always drink this while watching the annual Boxing Day shinty match in Dunkeld. Shinty is a Scottish sport not dissimilar to hockey, but with very few rules and sticks flying around the air left, right and centre. Needless to say, I keep to the side lines. The vodka is both warming and medicinal for the slightly fuzzy post-Christmas locals that gather in the masses to watch the match. I would also argue that it takes the edge off what can become quite a ferocious spectacle.

You are best to pick your sloes after the first frost; according to my mum this helps them break down when infusing the vodka. Alternatively, you can freeze them yourself, overnight, before using. I would always recommend doubling up this recipe, as you will be surprised by how quickly you can drink the stuff.

Makes 1 litre (34 fl oz/4 cups)

500 g (1 lb 1½ oz) sloes
750 g (1 lb 10½ oz/3 cups) vodka
350 g (12½ oz/1¾ cups) caster (superfine) sugar
3 sprigs of thyme (optional)

In a large 2 litre (68 fl oz/8 cup) bottle or jar, combine all the ingredients and shake well to help the sugar dissolve. You will need to shake it a least 3 times a week to encourage the sloes to break down. We leave our vodka to infuse for 8–12 weeks, but taste it as you go and simply strain once you are happy with the flavour. Once strained, store in a clean jar, with a sprig of fresh thyme. It will keep for a year or so.

Elderflower Cordial

24 flowers. 2oz citric acid
2½ lbs sugar 2½ pt boiling water
2 lemons thinly sliced

Make light syrup. cool
stir in other ingredients.
leave for 2 days. Stirring
occasionally strain through
muslin. dilute to taste

CORDIAL BY THE GALLON

Our favourite combinations are peach and thyme, rhubarb and ginger, blackcurrant and lemon verbena, and lemongrass and lime (use four lemongrass sticks, bashed, in place of the fruit).

Makes 750 ml (51 fl oz/3 cups)

550 g (1 lb 3½ oz/2¼ cups) water
450 g (1 lb/2¼ cups) caster
    (superfine) sugar
2 citrus fruit (lemon, orange or lime), sliced

450 g (1 lb) fruit (berries, rhubarb,
    stone fruit), sliced
thumb-sized piece of ginger
    (optional, but recommended)
25 g (1 oz) herbs or infusions (rosemary,
    thyme, lemon verbena, mint)

Bring the water and sugar to the boil in a deep saucepan over a medium heat. You want all the sugar to dissolve fully, leaving a clear liquid.

Add the rest of the ingredients to the pan and boil for a further 4–5 minutes, then set aside to cool. Cover and leave for 1–2 days to infuse. Once infused, strain into a sterilised glass bottle (see page 187). Keep in the refrigerator for up to 1 month.

ROMA'S ELDERFLOWER CORDIAL

The original recipe by my sweet great aunt Roma Robertson. There was nothing better when we were wee than running around her garden in the glorious Symington sunshine. We would only stop to drink vast quantities of this mixed with fizzy water. We still have a very splattered well-used copy of this recipe in her handwriting at home. I weigh this in pounds and ounces in her memory.

Makes 2 litres (70 fl oz/8 cups)

1.1 kg (2 lb 8 oz/5½ cups) caster
    (superfine) sugar

1.5 litres (51 fl oz/6 cups) boiling water
24 large elderflower heads
50 g (2 oz) citric acid
2 lemons, thickly sliced

Her exact method, below, is uncomplicated and non-fussy. Just like it should be.

'Make light syrup, cool. Stir in other ingredients. Leave for 2 days, stirring occasionally. Strain through muslin. Dilute to taste.'

9. HIGH TEA

Early evening

The evening begins to draw in and light darkens slightly. It is time for something a little more special. Bakes to be cherished and time committed to. Celebrate the end of the day on a high note.

BLOOD ORANGE MERINGUE PIES

One very hot summer's day, I tried to make a hundred of these tart cases in the shop, while we were very busy. Needless to say, it was a mammoth task. Though a little fiddly, these are well worth the effort and make for a delicious and unique afternoon tea or pudding. To make a lemon meringue pie, simply substitute the orange juice for lemon.

This curd is deliciously creamy and spoonable – I will be astounded if you want to make any other method of curd from now on. We certainly haven't. See recipe picture overleaf.

Makes 12 tartlets

1 batch of Sweet pastry (see page 228)
plain (all-purpose) flour, for dusting

for the blood orange curd
200 g (7 oz/¾ cup) blood orange juice

zest of 4 blood oranges
4 eggs
200 g (7 oz/1 cup) caster (superfine) sugar
300 g (10½ oz) unsalted butter, cubed

to finish
1 quantity of Italian meringue (see page 227)

Begin by making the blood orange curd as it needs plenty of time to chill and set before it is ready to use. Weigh out the blood orange juice, zest, eggs and caster sugar into a heatproof bowl set over a pan of simmering water. Whisk the mixture constantly until it reaches 80°C (175°F) on a digital thermometer. The temperature is key because the eggs need to be fully cooked in order for the finished cream to set with the correct consistency. Please don't skip this step.

Once the mixture comes to temperature, strain through a fine sieve to remove the zest and achieve a silky texture. Either transfer the mixture into the bowl of a food processor or use a stick blender to incorporate the butter into the hot mixture. You want to blend it in slowly, so add it piece by piece, making sure it gets fully incorporated.

When all of the butter has been added and the curd is fully blended, pour into an airtight container. Press a layer of cling film (plastic wrap) onto the surface of the cream to prevent a skin forming on top and refrigerate for at least 4 hours, although ideally overnight, until set but still spreadable. It will keep well in the refrigerator for up to 1 week.

Preheat the oven to 160°C (320°F/Gas 4).

Remove the rested pastry from the refrigerator and roll out on a lightly floured work surface, until 2–3 mm (⅛ in) thick. Cut into 12 large discs, then use to line 8 cm (3 in) tart rings. Trim off any excess, then place on a lined baking (cookie) sheet. Line each tart with a piece of crumpled greaseproof paper and fill with rice or lentils. Crumpling the paper makes it more pliable and softer, so less likely to damage or break the pastry. Smaller grains work best for this, as the cases are quite delicate and can be damaged easily. They are also far cheaper and can be used time and time again.

Blind bake the tart shells for roughly 15 minutes before carefully removing the rice and greaseproof paper and baking for a further 10 minutes, or until the inside is evenly baked and deep golden brown. Don't be afraid to cook them for longer than you would normally expect to – the cases have to hold up to high-moisture toppings so the crisper the better. Baking directly on the baking sheet helps with this as well. Once cooked, remove the tart ring gently and set aside to cool. These cases will keep well in an airtight container for up to 2 weeks.

When you are ready to assemble (always do this on the day of eating, otherwise the tart cases will go soft), remove the curd from the refrigerator and spoon into the cases. Use a small offset palette knife to smooth the surface and scrape off any excess.

Pipe the meringue on top and use another palette knife to swirl the meringue to form a pretty 'swoosh'. Blow torch the topping to set. These are best enjoyed on the day.

Blood orange meringue pies

CHOCOLATE PRALINE TARTLETS

Though this process seems long and potentially daunting you will end up with a massive vat or praline paste at the end, which alone it worth the time and energy. Drizzle any excess paste on good vanilla ice cream or spread onto the humble chocolate digestive for the ultimate after-dinner sweet treat. Almost but not quite as classy as these tartlets... Pictured overleaf.

Makes 12

1 batch of Sweet pastry (see page 228)
plain (all-purpose) flour, for dusting

for the praline paste
400 g (14 oz/2 cups) caster (superfine) sugar
200 g (7 oz/1¼ cups) hazelnuts
pinch of salt
100 g (3½ oz/ scant ½ cup) cold water

for the chocolate filling
375 g (13¼ oz/1½ cups) double
    (heavy) cream
75 g (2½ oz) unsalted butter
225 g (8 oz) dark chocolate

to finish
100 g (3½ oz/scant ½ cup) double cream
100 g (3½ oz/½ cup) mascarpone
edible flowers, to decorate

Preheat the oven to 180ºC (350ºF/Gas 6).

Begin by making the praline paste. Grease and line a 20 × 30 cm (8 × 12 in) heatproof shallow dish. Weigh the sugar into a large frying pan (skillet) and place on a medium to high heat. This caramel method is what we call a dry method, i.e. there is no extra water added at this stage. I find this the most reliable, but by all means add a few tablespoons of water if you have had more success making a wet caramel. Once the sugar begins to melt around the edges of the pan, start swirling it from side to side making sure all the granules are evenly spread across the pan. If you have a mountain of sugar on one side, there is more of a risk your caramel will cook too quickly before the rest of it is dissolved. Do not be tempted to stir otherwise it will crystallise. Swirling is the best technique – your wrist will get a bit of a workout!

Meanwhile, roast your hazelnuts for 2–3 minutes in a separate shallow tray in the preheated oven, just until fragrant but not coloured. They will be placed directly into the hot caramel, so you don't want them to be too far gone as they continue to cook a little and release their oils in the pan.

Once the sugar is all dissolved and the caramel is an even consistency, cook until golden or amber in colour. The minute you have reached a deep caramel shade, add the toasted nuts and stir to coat. Pour onto your lined tray and allow to set and cool down, roughly 15–20 minutes. Once solid, cut into chunks and place in a food processor. Add the pinch of salt and blitz on high. For this first stage I blitz the praline for 10 minutes non-stop, or until the mixture is smooth. It will form a sand-like texture for most of this period and look like it will never come together, but stick with it. If you find the mixture or your machine is getting too hot, turn it off and leave it for 15 minutes or so until cooled. This will avoid it burning out. If you haven't had to turn the machine off at any point after 10 minutes, do so now. I then leave the paste to cool down a little. After 20 minutes, return to the machine and blitz again at a high speed. You should notice the paste becomes much looser and resembles a thick peanut butter. While the machine is running, trickle in the cold water. The mixture will initially thicken and become lumpy before forming a smooth, silky texture. Taste and adjust the salt if you feel it is required or blitz a little more if it still has a slight graininess. Once completely smooth, pour into an airtight container and store in the refrigerator for up to 1 month. This recipe makes far more than is required for the tartlets, but it does require a bit of work and as it tastes so good and stores just as well you would be daft not to bulk up!

Remove the rested pastry from the refrigerator and roll out on a lightly floured work surface, until 2–3 mm (⅛ in) thick. Cut into 12 large discs, then use to line 8 cm (3 in) tart rings. Trim off any excess, then place on a lined baking (cookie) sheet. Line each tart with a piece of crumpled greaseproof paper and fill with rice or lentils. Crumpling the paper makes it more pliable and softer so less likely to damage or break the pastry. Smaller grains work best for this as the cases are quite delicate and can be damaged easily. They are also far cheaper and can be used time and time again.

Reduce the oven temperature to 160°C (320°F/Gas 4).

Blind bake the tart shells for roughly 15 minutes before carefully removing the rice and greaseproof paper and baking for a further 10 minutes, or until the inside is evenly baked and deep golden brown. Don't be afraid to cook them for longer than you would normally expect to – the cases have to hold up to high-moisture toppings so the crisper the better. Baking directly on the baking sheet helps with this as well. Once cooked, remove the tart ring gently and set aside to cool. These cases will keep well in an airtight container for up to 2 weeks.

When ready to assemble (ideally a few hours before eating), make your chocolate filling. Heat the butter and double cream together in a small saucepan and remove from the heat just before it boils. Chop the chocolate into fairly small and even pieces, then add the chocolate to the hot cream mixture. Whisk to combine and pour into a plastic jug (pitcher). Transfer some of the praline paste into a piping (pastry) bag and pipe rounds onto the base of each tartlet. You don't want to add too much as it is quite sweet, but enough so you have a thin layer on the bottom of the tart. Pour the chocolate filling directly on top while still hot. Transfer your tarts into the refrigerator for roughly 1–2 hours, or until set.

Just before serving, whip the double cream with the mascarpone until soft peaks form. Gently spoon onto the edge of the tart then top with an edible flower. We like using big blousy pale flowers as they look brilliant against the dark chocolate. Serve immediately.

Chocolate praline tartlets

Strawberry and tonka bean entremets

STRAWBERRY AND TONKA BEAN ENTREMETS

I was a big fan of a patisserie called Poppy & Sebastian based in London, that has now sadly closed down. Their creations were whimsical and simply beautiful in my eyes, and I spent a long time trying to recreate their entremets in as simple and as classy a fashion as they did. This is my version, and something we still do in the bakery from time to time when I can summon the energy and time. These are best when the strawberries are sweet, local and bursting with sunshine. A truly special form of baking. Pictured on page 209.

Makes 12 tartlets

1 batch of Sweet pastry (see page 228)
extra flour, for dusting
400–500 g (14 oz–1 lb 1½ oz) strawberries
2 tablespoons caster (superfine) sugar
2 tablespoons cognac

for the bavarois
4 gelatine leaves
150 g (5¼ oz/¾ cup) caster
    (superfine) sugar
300 g (10½ oz/1⅓ cup) double
    (heavy) cream
1 tonka bean, grated finely
600 g (1 lb 5 oz/2½ cups) yoghurt

for the mirror glaze
4 gelatine leaves
200 g (7 oz/1 cup) caster (superfine) sugar
125 g (4½ oz/½ cup) water
200 g (7 oz/¾ cup) double (heavy) cream
100 g (3½ oz) white chocolate,
    finely chopped
white food colouring paste (optional)

to finish
1 tonka bean, to decorate
edible rose petals

Begin with the bavarois. Soak the gelatine leaves in water while you bring the sugar, half of the cream and the tonka bean to the boil in a saucepan, then remove from heat. Once the gelatine has softened, squeeze the excess water from the gelatine, add to cream mixture and stir until dissolved.

Place the yoghurt in a large bowl and mix until smooth, then add the cream mixture and mix again until smooth. Set aside to cool, whisking occasionally, until it begins to thicken. I often place the bowl in a sink of cold water to help this along. Make sure it doesn't set, however. Whisk the remaining cream until soft peaks form, then gently fold it into the cooled yoghurt mixture with a whisk. Divide between twelve 8 cm (3 in) round dome moulds, which will be the same diameter as your tart cases. I use silicon moulds as they are easier when it comes to removing the domes. Place in the freezer overnight.

Preheat the oven to 160ºC (320ºF/Gas 4).

Remove the rested sweet shortcrust pastry from the refrigerator and roll out on a lightly floured work surface, until 2–3 mm (⅛ in) thick. Cut into 12 large discs, then use to line 8 cm (3 in) tart rings. Trim off any excess then place on a lined baking (cookie) sheet. Line each tart with a piece of crumpled greaseproof paper and fill with rice or lentils. Crumpling the paper makes it more pliable and softer so less likely to damage or break the pastry. Smaller grains work best for this as the cases are quite delicate and can be damaged easily. They are also far cheaper and can be used time and time again.

Blind bake the tart shells for roughly 15 minutes before carefully removing the rice and greaseproof paper and baking for a further 10 minutes or until the inside is evenly baked and deep golden brown. Don't be afraid to cook them for longer than you would normally expect to – the cases have to hold up to high-moisture toppings so the crisper the better. Baking directly on the baking tray helps with this as well. Once cooked, remove the tart ring gently and set aside to cool. These cases will keep well in an airtight container for up to 2 weeks.

To make the mirror glaze, soak the gelatine leaves in a bowl of cold water for a couple of minutes. Put the sugar in a saucepan with the water and place over a high heat until the sugar has completely dissolved. Stir in the cream and boil for a few minutes. Remove from the heat, squeeze out the excess water from the soaked and softened gelatine leaves and add to the hot cream mixture.

Allow the cream mixture to cool for a few minutes, then stir in the white chocolate. Make sure the chocolate is chopped fairly evenly to help it melt well. Once the chocolate has melted, add the food colouring and whisk until completely combined. The glaze should be a lovely soft white colour and not too yellow.

Set aside to cool to room temperature for 15–20 minutes, stirring from time to time to stop it from developing a skin. You want the glaze to be cool enough that it won't melt the bavarois, but still be pourable and not starting to set. If the glaze does begin to set, melt it again gently over a low heat.

To glaze the bavarois, remove them from the freezer. Remove the moulds and place on a metal cooling rack set over a baking sheet. Pour over the glaze making sure it covers the domes evenly. Scrape any excess glaze off the bottom of the sheet and reuse as required. Allow the domes to sit for 30 minutes or so, or until the glaze sets and the middles have defrosted.

To assemble, chop the strawberries into small chunks, reserving a few for decoration, and toss together with the sugar and cognac. Set aside for 10 minutes to marinate. Spoon the strawberries into the tart cases (do this right before serving to stop the pastry from going soggy. If you need to prep ahead of time simply paint the inside of the case with a little melted white chocolate and this will stop any sogginess). Carefully place a dome on top of the strawberries making sure it is fairly level. If your dome is the right size it should meet the edge of the tartlet case. Place a quarter of a strawberry on the top and grate a little more tonka bean over the top of the dome. Finish with a rose petal. Serve immediately.

POMEGRANATE AND RASPBERRY FINANCIERS

Simple to make, financiers can be a perfect after-dinner treat, baked to order. Simply preheat the oven and keep the batter in the refrigerator until you need it. You can pre-grease the moulds as well and store in the refrigerator if you are feeling extra organised. They don't even need the fruit on top if you simply want a little sweetness to finish the meal. This recipe truly is a blank canvas for ideas.

Makes 24

180 g (6½ oz) butter, plus extra for greasing
4 eggs
150 g (5¼ oz/¾ cup) caster (superfine) sugar
20 g (1½ tablespoons) muscovado sugar
pinch of salt
100 g (3½ oz/¾ cup) plain (all-purpose) flour
1¼ teaspoons baking powder
80 g (3 oz/½ cup) ground almonds

20 g (4 teaspoons) honey
250 g (8¾ oz) raspberries,
    plus extra to serve (optional)
seeds from ½ pomegranate,
    plus extra to serve (optional)

to serve
warmed honey, for brushing
icing (confectioner's) sugar, for dusting
mascarpone (optional)

Grease the financier moulds with melted butter and chill in the refrigerator. Using a spatula, mix the eggs, sugars and a pinch of salt in a bowl until combined. Sift the flour and baking powder into the bowl and add the almonds. Whisk into the mixture until well combined.

Melt the butter and honey together in a pan over a low heat. While stirring, pour the mix into the bowl, making sure it is well incorporated. Cover and leave to rest in the refrigerator for 30 minutes or overnight.

Preheat the oven to 160ºC (320ºF/Gas 4).

When the financier mix has rested, spoon into a piping (pastry) bag. Pipe the mix half way up each mould. Top with two raspberries each and a few pomegranate seeds and cook for 10–15 minutes until lightly golden brown.

Remove from the oven and allow to sit for 5 minutes before removing from the mould. Brush generously with warm honey and either serve warm dusted with icing sugar or at room temperature with more pomegranate seeds sprinkled on top, a little mascarpone and a half slice of raspberry. These are best eaten on the day of baking, but can be made to order as the mix stores well in the refrigerator.

WALNUT AND VANILLA ÉCLAIRS

Éclairs experienced a bit of a makeover a few years ago and suddenly have found themselves as fashionable, well-put-together puddings again, as opposed to the softer, more sorry pastries they had become. When topped with gold leaf and a mirror glaze I think they have rightfully earned their way back onto the modern-day menu.

Makes 8

for the choux pastry
100 g (3½ oz/scant ½ cup) water
100 g (3½ oz/scant ½ cup) whole
   (full-fat) milk
100 g (3½ oz) unsalted butter, diced
25 g (1½ tablespoons) caster
   (superfine) sugar
¼ teaspoon salt
150 g (5¼ oz/generous 1 cup) plain
   (all-purpose) flour
3 large eggs

for the mirror glaze
4 gelatine leaves
100 g (3½ oz/scant ½ cup) water

200 g (7 oz/1 cup) caster (superfine) sugar
200 g (7 oz/¾ cup) double (heavy) cream
100 g (3½ oz) white chocolate,
   finely chopped
1 teaspoon vanilla bean paste
white food colouring (optional)

for the crème légère
350 g (12½ oz/1½ cups) double
   (heavy) cream
½ quantity of Crème pât (see page 228)

to finish
50 g (1¾ oz/¼ cup) walnuts, toasted
   and chopped
gold leaf, to decorate (optional)

To make the glaze, soak the gelatine leaves in a bowl of cold water for a couple of minutes. Put the sugar in a saucepan with the water and place on a high heat until the sugar has completely dissolved. Stir in the cream and boil for a couple of minutes, then remove from the heat, squeeze out the excess water from the soaked and softened gelatine leaves and add to the hot cream mixture.

Allow the cream mixture to cool for a few minutes, then stir in the white chocolate and vanilla. Make sure the chocolate is chopped fairly evenly to help it melt well. Once the chocolate has melted, add the food colouring and whisk until completely combined. The glaze should be a lovely soft white colour and not too yellow. Set aside to cool to room temperature for 15–20 minutes, stirring from time to time to stop it from developing a skin. If the glaze does begin to set, melt it again gently over a low heat.

Preheat the oven to 180ºC (350ºF/Gas 6). Grease and line 2 baking (cookie) sheets.

Continued overleaf

To make the choux pastry, weigh the water, milk, butter, sugar and salt into a large saucepan and place over a medium-high heat. Whisk together until the butter has melted and the whole mixture comes to the boil. Remove the pan from the heat and add the flour straight into the pan, beating vigorously with a wooden spoon until your batter comes together to form a dough. It will be quite tough initially, but it will eventually bind together. Place the pan back on the heat, stirring constantly for about 2–3 minutes. This is in order to cook the flour. Tip the dough into a large bowl and set aside for 5 minutes to cool a little. Using an electric mixer, add the eggs to the bowl one at a time, beating constantly until smooth and fully incorporated. The resulting dough should have a slight gloss and, when lifted with a wooden spoon from the bowl, will form a deep 'V' shape.

Place the choux pastry into a piping (pastry) bag fitted with either a star or a plain nozzle. Pipe lengths of roughly 10–12 cm (4–5 in). Bake in the preheated oven for roughly 20 minutes, or until golden brown and crisp. Turn off the oven and allow the pastries to dry out for about 10 minutes before removing. Set aside to cool.

For the crème légère, whisk the cream until thickened. Gently fold in the crème pât, then whisk until thickened and lump free. Transfer to a piping bag fitted with a ruffle nozzle.

To assemble, cut the éclairs in half. Dunk the top half into the thickened glaze and coat well. Place on a wire rack to allow any excess to drip off. Once the glaze has stopped dripping, sprinkle with some chopped toasted walnuts down the middle. Pipe the crème légère in ruffles down the middle of the éclair. Top with more walnuts before placing the glazed lid on top. Finish with a small piece of gold leaf, if you fancy it.

LORRAINE

Lorraine has visited from day one and works selling all manner of kitchenware in the nearby shop, Kettles, which we often frequent. She is famous for her cheery smile and also her coffee order which is made in 'Lorraine's mug', of course. It comprises a single shot of espresso, two sweeteners, and hot milk to the top, finished off with a marshmallow and chocolate. Everyone at the bakery knows Lorraine's mug. She once said the main reason she visited the bakery was for the chat: 'It's a joy whether you are all hungover or not!'

What do you think of when you think of Aran?
I think of family, community and excellent marshmallows. I will be coming to this glorious establishment, come rain or shine, for as long as I can.

If you were a bakery good what would you be?
My coffee! Or the apple and olive oil cake – a bit sweet and also light and airy… make of that what you will!

Who is your favourite Aran employee?
Hebe. You are all lovely but me and Hebe have got history…

10. GLOAMING

Dusk, bakery closed

noun, literary, meaning 1. twilight, dusk,
2. 'hundreds of lights are already shimmering in the gloaming'

The end of the day, lights off. Shop swept, dishes done, cakes long gone. We celebrate often, with drinks, long conversations where most of us are horizontal with exhaustion, trips to the pub, slapdash dinners and many a cheese toasty. Plans for the gym are often brushed aside for gin and, before we know it, bed beckons and we begin the carnage all over again.

WHAT A PEAR

For Angus and Scott, the duo that started it all.

Serves 4

250 g (8¾ oz) pears, ripe and skin removed, plus extra to garnish
150 g (5½ oz/⅔ cup) white wine
50 g (1¾ oz/¼ cup) sugar syrup
100 g (3½ oz/scant ½ cup) brandy
50 g (1¾ oz/¼ cup) lemon juice
ice
mint leaves, to serve

In a food processor, blitz the pears until you have a smooth purée. Add the wine, sugar syrup, brandy and lemon juice, then blitz again until combined. Pour half into a cocktail shaker with a little ice and shake well. Double strain into a glass of your choice with a little more ice, then repeat with the rest of the mixture. Garnish with a fan of sliced pear and some mint leaves.

OLD FASHIONED ARAN

This is my go-to drink. I spent a lot of time debating as to whether I preferred a Negroni, but after a month of drinking these at our local pub, The Taybank, my mind was well and truly made up.

Serves 1

1 teaspoon Demerara sugar
50 g (1¾ oz/¼ cup) whisky*
4 dashes of bitters - if you have 2 varieties,
    use half and half, as this will help the flavour,
    but if not Angostura bitters will work well
1 strip of orange peel
ice

In a mixing glass, muddle together the sugar and the whisky for a few minutes. Add the bitters and a few cubes of ice along with a strip of orange peel. Stir together, then strain into your preferred glass – it's not essential to use an old fashioned glass – with a few cubes of fresh ice. Remove the orange peel, twist over the glass then add to garnish. Serve immediately.

I am more than happy to use Scottish whisky in an Old Fashioned, although I know some people will say it's sacrilege. If you find it offensive, I recommend Maker's Mark as an alternative.

THE JULIA

In honour of our bakery manager (and saviour) Julia, who famously invented her namesake coffee, which consists of one shot of espresso, half hot water, half steamed milk and finally a splash of oat milk to top it off. She would serve it in a wee flat-white glass, and everyone became hooked on them. Truly, we would be nowhere without her (and maybe a few of these...).

Serves 1

50 g (1¾ oz/¼ cup) vodka
25 g (1 oz/2 tablespoons) coffee liqueur (we use Kahlúa)
25 g (1 oz/2 tablespoons) espresso
ice
oat milk (optional, we use Minor Figures,
    but any barista-standard oat milk
    would work)
coffee beans, to serve

Put all the ingredients apart from the coffee beans into a cocktail shaker, give it a good shake, then strain into a Martini glass and serve decorated with a coffee bean or two.

BASICS

LEMON ICING

Makes enough to ice 2-3 loaf cakes

300 g (10½ oz/2⅓ cups) icing (confectioner's) sugar
50 g (1¾ oz/¼ cup) freshly squeezed lemon juice,
    plus extra if you need to loosen

Beat the ingredients together in a mixing bowl until lump-free and smooth. Use immediately or store in the refrigerator for up to 2 weeks. You can use other citrus juice; however, bear in mind you may need to add a little more or less juice depending on the variety.

BUTTERCREAM

Makes enough to ice 2-3 round 20 cm (8 in) cakes

500 g (1 lb 1½ oz) unsalted butter
1 kg (2 lb 3 oz/8 cups) icing
    (confectioner's) sugar
1 teaspoon vanilla bean paste

Melt 125 g (4½ oz) butter in a small saucepan. Cube the remaining butter and add to a free-standing mixer. Pour the hot butter over the top and whisk the butter on a high speed until completely silky and pale in colour. If your butter is very soft you can skip this step; however, living in Scotland and working in a cold kitchen, more months than not this is a brilliant technique when it comes to lump-free buttercream.

Add the icing sugar along with the vanilla. Beat on a high speed for 5 minutes until it becomes pale and fluffy again. If you feel this is taking a while, you can add a wee splash of boiling water to loosen and soften the mixture. Only use once white in colour and light and airy in texture. Store at room temperature for up to 1 week or in the refrigerator for up to 2 weeks.

SWISS BUTTERCREAM

Makes enough to ice 2-3 round 20 cm (8 in) cakes

4 egg whites
300 g (10½ oz/1½ cups) caster (superfine) sugar
400 g (14 oz) unsalted butter, cubed and softened
1 teaspoon vanilla extract
¼ teaspoon salt

Weigh the eggs whites and the sugar into a metal or glass bowl. I like to do this in the metal bowl of my free-standing mixer as you will be using this later on, but you can of course use any heatproof bowl. Place the bowl over a pan half filled with water and bring to the boil. Whisk the eggs and sugar together over the heat until you have a white, creamy mixture that is warm and smooth when rubbed between two fingers (this means the sugar has completely dissolved).

Remove from the heat and using a free-standing mixer or hand-held mixer, whisk together for 10 minutes or until cooled, pale and glossy. Turn the mixer down to a medium speed and add the butter, cube by cube. You want to do this slowly so that the mixture doesn't split. It should take you roughly 5 minutes to add all of the butter. Finally, add the vanilla and salt and beat until you have a glossy spreadable mixture. Use immediately or store in the refrigerator for up to 2 weeks. If you are making this ahead, you will need to bring the mixture to room temperature and beat again on a high speed in order to make it silky again.

ITALIAN MERINGUE

Makes enough for 12 tartlets

200 g (7 oz/1 cup) caster (superfine) sugar
100 g (3½ oz/scant ½ cup) water
200 g (7 oz) egg whites

In a saucepan, bring the sugar and water to the boil at the same time as placing the egg whites into a very clean bowl of a free-standing mixer.

Once the sugar syrup reaches the temperature of 110°C (230°F) on a sugar thermometer, begin to whisk the eggs on a high speed. Once the sugar reaches 118°C (244°F), remove from the heat.

When the eggs are thick and glossy, pour the hot syrup into the mixer and turn down to a medium speed. You want to do this slowly and steadily so as not to lose too much air. Continue to whisk until the mixture has cooled and is thick and glossy. Use immediately or store in the refrigerator in an airtight container for up to 1 week.

FRANGIPANE

Makes enough for a 30 cm (12 in) tart

250 g (8¾ oz) unsalted butter
250 g (8¾ oz/2¼ cups) caster (superfine) sugar
200 g (7 oz/1¼ cups) ground almonds
100 g (3½ oz/¾ cup) self-raising flour
2 eggs

In a mixing bowl, beat all the ingredients together until light, pale and fluffy. Store in the refrigerator until required. It will keep for up to 3 days.

CHOCOLATE GANACHE

Makes enough to ice 1 Devil's food cake

150 g (5½ oz/⅔ cup) double (heavy) cream
25 g (1 oz/1½ tablespoons) golden syrup
1 teaspoon vanilla bean paste
150 g (5½ oz) dark chocolate (anything above 54% cocoa solids), roughly chopped or in chip form

In a saucepan, heat the cream, golden syrup and vanilla until just about to boil; make sure you watch it carefully as it can boil over before you know it. Remove from the heat, allow to cool for 2 minutes, then add the chocolate. Whisk together until smooth and glossy. Fill a sink with ice and cold water and place the pan in the cool water whisking regularly until the mixture has thickened and is spreadable. Store in the refrigerator for up to 2 weeks, gently melting when required.

OAT CRUMBLE

Makes enough for 2 loaf cakes

100 g (3½ oz/¾ cup) plain (all-purpose) flour
50 g (1¾ oz/⅔ cup) rolled oats
100 g (3½ oz) unsalted butter
50 g (1¾ oz/¼ cup) caster (superfine) or muscovado sugar
50 g (1¾ oz/¼ cup) chopped hazelnuts, optional

In the bowl of a food processor, weigh out all of the ingredients and blitz them together on a high speed until the mixture resembles a crumble-like consistency. Scrape down and blitz again until you have a chunky mixture. Store in the refrigerator until required. Alternatively, you can freeze this mixture for up to 3 months and bake straight from frozen.

CRÈME PÂT

Makes enough for a batch of brioche buns

500 g (1lb 1½ oz/2 cups) whole (full-fat) milk
2 eggs
80 g (2½ oz/⅓ cup) caster (superfine) sugar
30 g (2 tablespoons) cornflour (cornstarch)
1 teaspoon vanilla bean paste

In a pan, warm the milk and remove from the heat just before it begins to boil. Meanwhile, whisk together the eggs, sugar and cornflour with the vanilla. Pour the hot milk over the egg mixture, whisking all the time.

Pour the combined mixture back into the pan and return to a low heat. Whisk the mixture continuously until it thickens up. Do not allow it to boil. Once thickened, pour into a heatproof airtight container. Press a piece of cling film (plastic wrap) on top to prevent a skin from forming. Allow to cool completely before placing the lid on top and storing in the refrigerator for up to 1 week.

SWEET PASTRY

Makes enough for a 30 cm (12 in) tart

250 g (8¾ oz) unsalted butter, cubed
500 g (1 lb 1½ oz/4 cups) plain (all-purpose) flour
200 g (7 oz/1⅔ cups) icing (confectioner's) sugar
1 egg

In the bowl of a food processor, weigh out all the ingredients and blitz on a high speed until the mixture resembles a crumble-like consistency. Stop the machine and scrape down the sides. Blitz again, stopping when the mixture combines and forms a dough. Alternatively, you can do this by hand, working the butter into the flour and icing sugar until you have a sand-like texture. Add the egg, then work gently to bring the dough together.

Once combined, flatten into a rough rectangle 2 cm (1 in) thick. This helps chill the dough faster and makes it easier for you to roll out. Cover with cling film (plastic wrap) and rest in the refrigerator for at least 30 minutes. This will keep well in the refrigerator for up to 3 days.

SAVOURY PASTRY

Makes enough for a 30 cm (12 in) tart

250 g (8¾ oz) unsalted butter, cubed
250 g (8¾ oz/2 cups) wholemeal (wholewheat) flour
250g (8¾ oz/2 cups) plain (all-purpose) flour
1 teaspoon mixed dried herbs
salt and freshly ground black pepper
1 egg
2 tablespoons whole (full-fat) milk

In the bowl of a food processor, weigh out all the ingredients and blitz on a high speed until the mixture resembles a crumble-like consistency. Stop the machine and scrape down the sides. Blitz again, stopping when the mixture combines and forms a dough. Alternatively, you can do this by hand by working the butter into the flours, herbs and seasoning until you have a sand-like texture. Add the egg and milk, then work gently to bring the dough together.

Once combined, flatten into a rough rectangle 2 cm (1 in) thick. This helps chill the dough faster and makes it easier for you to roll out. Cover with cling film (plastic wrap) and rest in the refrigerator for at least 30 minutes. This will keep well in the refrigerator for up to 3 days.

STOCKISTS

IKEA
loaf tins, bakery utensils, cookie cutters
www.ikea.com

SOUS CHEF
tonka beans, pearl sugar, edible dried flowers
www.souschef.co.uk

NISBETS
bakery kit, cake tins, dough scrapers
www.nisbets.co.uk

POLKA PLANTS
brilliant trousers for ladies,
cooks and bakers alike
www.polkapants.com

BAKERY BITS
bread baskets, banneton liners,
bread knives, scorers
www.bakerybits.co.uk

LAKELAND
all baking decoration, including
food colouring and liners
www.lakeland.co.uk

MARRIAGES FLOUR
the flour we use everyday
www.flour.co.uk

GREENS OF DEVON
edible flowers, if you aren't lucky enough
to have a Dad, an Innes or a Heather locally
www.greensofdevon.com

WILKO
best source for multipacks of jam jars
www.wilko.com

TOAST
beautiful long-lasting linen aprons
www.toa.st

ACKNOWLEDGEMENTS

Since opening Aran we have learnt it takes a village to run a bakery. It seems you also require a village to write a book about it. James, all my love and thanks for letting a bakery take over our lives. Thank you for the laughter and the comic attempts at taking my mind off the anxiety of running a small business.

Mumma, the real boss. There would be no bakery without you and the aprons would certainly not be ironed. Thank you for your presence, support, advice and entertainment. The whole team love you excessively, but not quite as much as I do. Thank you for everything.

Dad, thank you for not expressing panic when I walked away from university for a second time, moved home and bought a shop and house with a man I barely knew. Thank you for your support, washing-up hours and complete honesty throughout. I love and adore you.

Hebe and Willow, I love you both. Thank you for working all hours and for bringing so much colour to a completely white bakery – how boring it would all be without you.

Granny Shedden and Granny and Grandpa Ross, thank you for supporting me as I ventured down this unconventional path.

And to Papa Shedden, although you didn't get to try any Aran baking, I really hope you would have loved it nearly as much as you loved a raisin biscuit from M&S. I miss you.

To the Shedden and the Ross clans, sorry I dropped off the face of the earth while getting Aran up and running, and then again while writing this book. I look forward to more adventures, antics and feasts ahead.

Laura, what a dream to do it all over again – you are completely marvellous and infuriatingly talented. Loads of love, thanks and big soppy hugs.

Rosie R, thank you for joining the craziness. your skills are unrivalled and I am truly lucky that you were the one translating my madness. What a treat to spend time with you.

Tab, I missed you so much and so adored being back in your presence again. To have your remarkable style and aesthetic on the team again was a real delight.

Jess, Kitty and Rosie F, a total pleasure to meet and work with you all. Thank you for your knacks for details, your insights and your blethering. How sweet to spend time with such kind souls.

Sam and Matt, thank you for silently grafting away amongst our constant squeals of excitement.

Kajal, right from day one you just got it. Thank you for making this book mean so much, and for reassuring me throughout. I cannot describe how wonderful it is to work with someone who cares as much as you do. You are one-in-a-million and an excellent pal.

To Stuart, your beautiful work is much appreciated. You captured the aesthetic and simplicity of Aran right from the start and I am thrilled with how brilliantly it all came together thanks to you.

Everyone at HG, thank you for your work behind the scenes. Thank you for taking my email rambles and making them mean something. Thank you for putting as much love into this book as I did.

To all our brilliant customers, past and present: Aran would not be where it is today without you. You have welcomed us into the community, travelled near and far to visit, and have made the experience nothing short of a pleasure. Thank you from the bottom of my heart for embracing us – the chaos and the carbs! We adore every single one of you.

To Team Aran – there are no adjectives powerful enough to let you all know how thankful I am. I am in a constant state of shock that we manage to open our doors every morning and I know that this is entirely down to all of your tirelessly hard graft. Thank you for running away to the circus with me.

And finally to Angus, who has been in on it since the start. It has meant so much to me that you ever even considered putting up with my total cluelessness, especially as it became increasingly apparent. Without your skill, experience and unwavering patience I really don't think we would be what we are today.

Published in 2019 by Hardie Grant Books,
an imprint of Hardie Grant Publishing

Hardie Grant Books (London)
5th & 6th Floors
52–54 Southwark Street
London, SE1 1UN

Hardie Grant Books (Melbourne)
Building 1, 658 Church Street
Richmond, Victoria 3121

hardiegrantbooks.com

British Library Cataloguing-in-Publication Data.
A catalogue record for this book is available from
the British Library.

Aran   ISBN: 978-1-78488-310-2
10 9 8 7 6 5 4 3

Publishing Director: Kate Pollard
Commissioning Editor: Kajal Mistry
Junior Editors: Bex Fitzsimons; Eila Purvis
Design and Art Direction: Stuart Hardie
Photographer: Laura Edwards
Photography Assistants: Sam Harris; Matthew Hague
Food Stylists: Rosie Ramsden; Jess Dennison
Food Styling Assistants: Rosie French; Kitty Cole
Prop Stylist: Tabitha Hawkins
Editor: Eve Marleau
Proofreader: Emily Preece-Morrison
Indexer: Cathy Heath
Cover Retouching: Butterfly Creatives
Colour reproduction by p2d
Printed and bound in China by Leo Paper Products Ltd.